KT-165-840

MAN WITH
TWO DOGS

MAN WITH TWO DOGS

A Breath of Fresh Air from Scotland

ANGUS WHITSON

BLACK & WHITE PUBLISHING

First published 2007
by Black & White Publishing Ltd
99 Giles Street, Edinburgh EH6 6BZ

3 5 7 9 10 8 6 4 2 07 08 09 10 11

ISBN 13: 978 1 84502 153 5
ISBN 10: 1 84502 153 3

Typeset by RefineCatch Ltd, Bungay, Suffolk
Printed and bound by MPG Books Ltd, Bodmin, Cornwall

My thanks to *The Courier & Advertiser*
for giving me the chance to enjoy myself so
much and Graham Lang whose witty
illustrations embellish the stories.

Pictures by niallbenvie.com

Visit the 'Man with two dogs' website to see
every Saturday article published in *The Courier*.
Updated each week.
www.manwithtwodogs.com

For my mother and father and my family and grandchildren – especially the Doyenne who patiently puts up with my continued nonsenses.

Contents

Introduction

2003

Winter

As Good as a Rest   3

Spring

Hormone Horror   7
From the Doyenne's Kitchen –
       Roadkill Pie   9
Struggling On   10
Seashore and Salmon   12

Summer

Miscellany   17
Elderflower Cordial   19
From the Doyenne's Kitchen –
       Elderflower Cordial   21
Midlothian Expedition   23
Wildlife in the Workplace   25

Autumn

In the Midst of Life . . .   27
The Broch   29
Countryside Musings   31
Saint and the Cheese   34
From the Doyenne's Kitchen –
       Chocolate Cake   36
       Auntie Win Biscuits   38

2003–2004

Winter

Cows May Fly	43
Down by the Riverside	46
Wooden House	48
Self-Sufficiency	50
From the Doyenne's Kitchen –	
Ann's Marmalade	52

Spring

Strange Tongues	55
Historical Walks	58
Death of a Friend	59
Big Tree Country	63

Summer

Man's Best Friend	67
Celtic Culture and Salmon Fishers	69
Ecological	72
Border Tales	75

Autumn

Sunshine	77
From the Doyenne's Kitchen –	
Rowan and Apple Jelly	79
Healthy Eating	80
Glen Roadman	82

2004–2005

Winter

Miniature Train	87
Native Scottish Wildcat	89

Seashore and Semi-Precious Stones   91

Spring
The Wild Geese Depart   95
Border Country and Recycling a Bridge   97
The Pirate and the Pig   100
Ancestors and Orkney   102

Summer
Legacy of the RNLI   105
Scottish Painters and Scottish Seals   108
Inka and Whisky   109
Genealogy   111

Autumn
High Jinks in Marykirk   115
Mixed Bag   117
Morris Dancing and Quails   119
J. M. Barrie writes *Peter Pan*   121

2005–2006

Winter
Wee Dappin   127
Golf Balls   129

Spring
Raptor Rapture and Green Sandpiper   133
Eels and Old Nick   135
Country Sports   137
Natural Remedies   140

Summer
Fishy Story   143
Silver Salmon – King of Fish   145

Thunder and Lightning   147
Swimming Moles   149

Autumn

Church Raptor   153
Prisoner in a Jelly Factory   155
From the Doyenne's Kitchen –
           Bramble Jelly   157
Low Fungi and Tall Trees   158
Scotland Invented Whisky   160
From the Doyenne's Kitchen –
           Sloe Gin   161
Recycling the Biker   164

2006–2007

Winter

Nature, the Great Provider   169
From the Doyenne's Kitchen –
           Rook Pie   171
Goose Fever   172
Twitcher   174
From the Doyenne's Kitchen –
           Mince Pies   176
Cool Pictish Reverie   178
Burns Night and Dancing Haggis   180
Puzzle for the Squirrels   182

Introduction

I count myself lucky to have lived most of my adult life in the country, with doorstep access to the countryside and nature. I was fortunate, too, to marry a girl who, although raised in Bradford, had a great love of the Yorkshire Dales and shares my enthusiasm for the outdoors. We brought up our family in a rambling, retired Scottish manse in north Angus, on the east coast of Scotland, which lay at the end of a country road beyond which were fields and freedom. It delights us to see our daughter and sons now passing on their enthusiasm for country life to their own children.

It all started with my own parents who introduced my sister, Grizel, and me to sea and loch, river and glen and the hills and the sky on expeditions around Montrose and our home county of Angus and on holidays in the north-west of Scotland. Being out of doors was the important thing – the state of the weather less so.

Looking back, my father, who was a man of extremes, seemed to embody the attitude that, if it wasn't uncomfortable, it wasn't 'proper' fun. He must have sold us the idea pretty successfully because we seem to have accepted the discomforts, such as they were (perhaps our mother persuaded him to moderate his worst excesses), with good humour. If I didn't question his judgement then, I suspect I should most certainly do so now!

Both parents taught us to be enquiring and to appreciate and respect our surroundings and leave them in at least the same condition, or better, for those who came after.

For my own diversion, I started writing short articles about the things I saw and heard when out walking my two dogs. There have always been dogs in my life – the first two of the 'Man with Two Dogs' articles were Sheba, a black Labrador, and Macbeth, a West Highland White Terrier. Sheba died in 2004 and it was fourteen months before Inka, another black Lab, came to us in July 2005.

I was lucky in another respect. A chance conversation resulted in my being invited to send sample articles to the editor of *The Courier & Advertiser*, our local daily newspaper which is published by D. C. Thomson & Co. Ltd in Dundee. Quite to my delight, I was asked to contribute a regular Saturday countryside diary to the paper and 'Man with Two Dogs' was hatched.

Before e-mailing the pieces to *The Courier* for publication, each weekly contribution is submitted to my wife, the Doyenne, for 'signing off'. Why 'Doyenne', I'm often asked. Continued reference to 'my wife' might eventually make her seem remote and the alternatives were unsatisfactory. A doyenne is 'a most respected or prominent woman in a particular field'. How better can I characterise that most respected and prominent person who is my wife?

Scots and Yorkshire folk have much in common, not the least of which is a great flair as enterprising cooks. My generous shadow is surely testament to the Doyenne's kitchen skills and some of her recipes appear here alongside the articles where they are mentioned.

Friends tell us they no longer need to see us as they can catch up with our activities every weekend in the paper. In the fish shop one day, a regular reader confided to the Doyenne that she reads my article in *The Courier* each Saturday morning even before she reads the deaths column! One should always accept compliments in the spirit in which they are given.

Every family has its own stories which are passed down the generations. Writing the weekly articles has recalled all sorts of memories that might otherwise have remained forgotten. So 'Man with Two Dogs' looks like being my legacy to our family and grandchildren, who regularly feature in the column. I also write about my father and mother – I wish they were still here to call on for their memories and to check events. And then there are my Loanhead aunties who surface from time to time – I had two of them and they have proved invaluable as unassailable sources of authority when I have been challenged on matters of fact!

I have the greatest fun writing my weekly column and have benefited from the disciplines of the daily dog walking and meeting my weekly deadline for *The Courier*. Readers too have played their part by kindly writing in response to queries or to tell me about their own experiences and sometimes to correct me! Others call with items they think may be of interest.

Comments that 'Man with Two Dogs' is not only entertaining but that 'you learn things too' have been very encouraging. But perhaps it's all best summed up by the reader who wrote to me, addressing the envelope:

The Man with Two Dogs
(Lucky Man, Lucky Dogs)

2003

Winter

The snowdrops are still going strong and the daffodils are growing well. In the more sheltered parts of the garden, they have reached the 'pencil' stage. This is the point when the immature buds point skywards like a pencil, before the blooms fall over in their characteristic droop.

Dogs enjoy a change just as much as we humans. Like us, they get bored by the same walk every day with no variation to stimulate them so we are fortunate having such a choice of walks close to home. But a visit to son James and his family at Gorebridge, near Edinburgh, meant new sights, sounds and smells for Sheba and Macbeth. Macbeth is thoroughly sociable so meeting new dogs is a proper treat for him.

With the other set of 'out-laws' (daughter-in-law's parents), we took an extended-family walk over the Braid Hills golf course which lies on the south side of Edinburgh. This is a city greatly blessed with numerous green spaces. There is a regular population of small mammals and bird life living in the broom- and whin-covered hillocks round which the golf course is built.

Two hunting kestrels were quartering over the ground oblivious to us humans and our dogs. We are obviously just another part of the landscape to be taken account of. There were rabbit tracks in the patches of snow which still hadn't thawed in the shaded parts of the course. I saw fox droppings which probably meant an untimely end for some of the rabbits. Urban foxes are a common sight in most cities nowadays.

I've been missing the calls of the geese in recent weeks. For me, they are one of the authentic voices of winter. They haven't been around in the same numbers as last winter. The farmers won't mind because they do so much damage to winter-growing crops. However, on the car journey to Edinburgh we saw three to four hundred greylag geese feeding on stubbles close to Kinross, not far from Vane Farm Nature Reserve.

I had a call from an enthusiastic country-life observer. He had been walking his two dogs along the bank of the River South Esk opposite Arrats Mill, which lies about halfway between Brechin and the river's entry into Montrose Basin. He had seen a seal in the river with what he judged to be a seven-pound salmon in its mouth.

I discussed this with an old friend, Charlie Lorimer, who has known the river all his life. He confirmed that it's not frequent but nor is it unknown for seals to swim so far up the river. He has seen them sunning themselves on the gravel banks by the Bridge of Dun. But, like me, he had never seen one flourishing its lunch like a trophy.

I've noticed there's a fever about salmon stories that produces a frenzy of optimism in their telling. A seven-pound salmon, indeed! Not even Macbeth fell for that fishy tail.

Spring

March - Hormone Horror

Dead pheasants lying by the roadsides have mostly been knocked down by speeding cars. It's usually cock pheasants which are probably beginning to fizz with excess hormones as their breeding season approaches. It must be difficult to be so gorgeous and not let it go to your head – with savage results in some cases.

In years past, there was less traffic and it went slower so the carnage was less. Pheasants have never seemed the brainiest of birds and, although their minds are brimming with the joys of mating, they should give more thought to their mortality. Hitting a heavy cock pheasant can cause damage to your car out of all proportion to the size of the bird – dented bodywork and broken headlamps are not uncommon.

There's great excitement in this household as we have heard woodpeckers drumming away on nearby trees – only twice but it's a start. From what several kind readers have told me, the key to attracting these handsome birds to the garden is an unremitting menu of peanuts. I'm dreaming up a strategy of placing feeders on the edge of the woods closest to the garden and slowly moving them nearer and nearer to the house.

It's not often you see an unbroken rainbow but, after a particularly heavy thunderplump of rain, I saw a double rainbow although the colours of the upper one were not as intense as the lower. I just had to stop the car and look. I know the exact tree, in the exact field, where the end of the rainbow came down. At midnight, I shall be out there digging for the crock of gold my mother always promised me was buried at the foot of the rainbow.

Days are stretching out and the dawn chorus starts earlier. It's so much more of a pleasure to get out of bed and see the daylight breaking. There are still heavy frosts, though, to set the blood tingling when I take the dogs out first thing.

Time to start cutting the grass. It's aggravating the way it just grows straight back up again. And our neighbours all have 'bowling greens' in their front gardens which put me to shame.

I've noticed one or two new field fences on my travels. Not too notable a sight you might think but take a look at how many fields no longer have their familiar wire and post fence. There's no need for a fence if you don't have livestock to put in the field. After the foot and mouth troubles of 2001, many farms ceased to stock cattle and sheep altogether. Perhaps the new fences are an indication of farmers' revived confidence in the future.

Macbeth spotted a hen pheasant ahead of us and

was after it like lightning. By the time I caught up with him the bird was dead. It had severe injuries on its back, probably from being struck by a car, which would have prevented it from flying. I suspect the extra trauma of Macbeth was just too much for it and it died, quite literally, of fright.

From the Doyenne's Kitchen

ROADKILL PIE

My husband brings home dead pheasants and other roadside casualties which, thankfully, he is quite prepared to pluck, skin or otherwise cope with.

Roadkill pie, in our household, is made mostly from the breasts of pheasants picked up off the side of the road. Not just any old bird but the one that wasn't on that stretch of road when you went shopping and is there when you drive back!

The best parts of the bird are skinned and the breasts and thighs if they're not damaged, taken off. We keep a plastic box in the freezer with bits of game in it and, when we've collected enough, I have the makings of roadkill pie.

Method

Pan-fry the pheasant pieces in butter over a hot heat and then put them in a warm casserole dish while you fry sliced onions and mushrooms. Add a slug of white wine to the pan and cook quickly to burn off the alcohol. Add all this to the pheasants with some good stock and cook in a medium oven for about 40 minutes.

Roll out a piece of puff pastry, place an upturned pie dish on the pastry and cut round it. Place the pastry on a greased baking sheet and brush with beaten egg. Bake in a hot oven until puffy and golden brown. Stir some cream into the casserole and tip the contents into the pie dish. Pop the piece of cooked pastry on top, reheat and serve with mashed potatoes and carnip (i.e., carrots and turnip mashed together with butter).

PS An alternative is carsnip which is mashed carrot and parsnip.

April - Struggling On

The Highland cattle in the wildest parts of the Lake District seemed rather far from home – but there they were in a field beside the road at the foot of the Kirkstone Pass. The start of the Pass, which climbs from Ambleside and drops down into Ullswater, is known as The Struggle and it's easy to understand why. What a struggle it must have been for horses pulling carts up that terrible incline in the early days of the road. It can be compared with the hill up to Balintore Castle which lies to the west of Kirriemuir. My father called it the

Hill of a Hundred Horses because that was the number they say died hauling the stone to build the castle.

Flowering daffodils make yellow splashes of colour in the fields behind the house. These are not for picking – the bulbs will be lifted and sold for next spring's gardens and planters. There is an annual display of the flowers along the Kingsway bypass in Dundee. Several varieties have been planted and, as some die, more colour follows on, prolonging the cheery welcome to the city.

Smoke drifting across the hillside somewhere about Glen Lethnot, at the back of Brechin, was probably coming from muirburn. Gamekeepers burn old heather (muir or moor) to encourage new growth in the plants. The young shoots are the staple diet of grouse and, like us humans, the birds enjoy nothing better than fresh, organic food that needs no preparation.

Macbeth has just had his regular clip. It's hard to believe the change in him when we get him home – he's like something off the lid of a chocolate box and so different from his normal mobile midden state.

Sheba has been on painkillers and is moving much more comfortably, which is a relief. (She was elderly by this time and suffering from arthritis.) Hopefully she'll soon be able to jump in and out of the car unaided once more. I was beginning to think I would blow a gasket if I had to heave her about the place much longer.

I had a phone call from Arthur Grewar, who is a keen observer of nature from the cab of his tractor. He had seen a leveret, or young hare, lying in its 'flap', which is

11

just a depression in the grass that the hare flattens itself into and can practically disappear from sight.

We talk of 'mad March hares' performing their courtship rituals in the month of March so this youngster must have been conceived and born quite outwith the normal timetable. Perhaps the mild winter weather we're experiencing these days fools the parent animals into thinking it's time to breed far ahead of the customary cycle.

While we – the Doyenne and I, that is – were in the Lake District enjoying a family wedding and the wild party that followed, the dogs were having a rare old time at kennels on our neighbours' farm at home. But they still shower us with delirious greetings when we collect them.

Glancing out of the window I see a cock pheasant with a harem of four hens. He'll have his time cut out for himself shortly!

May - Seashore and Salmon

We – Macbeth and I, that is – went for a long tramp on St Cyrus beach just north of Montrose. He'd never seen the beach before and, as the tide was out, he was absolutely stunned by the amount of space. For several minutes, he didn't quite know which way to go and ran around in circles trying to get some sort of bearings.

I lay down on my stomach to get an idea of perspective from his eye level. Small wonder he was astonished – it just went on and on with no apparent end. I couldn't see Scurdie Ness lighthouse, near Montrose, which is quite visible when standing up. And waves were a cause of some concern to him. But then, to Macbeth, a wave a foot high must look how the Red Sea looked when it rolled back on the pursuing Egyptians.

To get a better idea of your dog's life, lie down – or, like me, wobble – on your stomach to appreciate what your pet sees.

We share strangely different lives with our dogs. Unlike them, we humans can't follow a scent, running on all fours and sniffing at the same time. The seashore wasn't too interesting for smells and we walked back to the car along the bents at the foot of the cliffs. The large number of rabbit holes and scrapings were much more fulfilling.

Trips to St Cyrus beach were a feature of my childhood. Along with other skinny children, we were thrust by insensitive mothers into the freezing sea, with the assurance that seawater was good for us. I don't remember the mothers sharing the benefits with their children.

I recall a lot more noise in the past – of seabirds up on the cliffs, especially at this nesting time. Perhaps it was late in the day and everything was settling down for the evening but I did expect to see and hear more.

We passed what I know as Beattie's Grave, a sheltered graveyard lying between the sand dunes and the cliffs, which recalls a tragic tale. George Beattie, a Montrose solicitor of undistinguished background, was rejected by the high-born daughter of a local laird. In his despair, he blew out his brains in the graveyard and is buried at the spot he died.

There are still salmon nets along the beach to catch the migrant salmon returning to their mother rivers to spawn. Until recently, the bay at St Cyrus featured the traditional arrow-shaped stake nets, or fly nets, which were developed over generations of experience and were a most effective method of catching the King of Fish.

Nowadays, much smaller 'jumper' nets are used. They have the same arrowhead-shaped bag of net to catch the fish but can be operated by one man. It being Saturday, the nets were 'slapped'. Fishing is prohibited between 6 p.m. on Friday till 6 a.m. on Monday and the nets must be left open for the salmon to escape during this time.

Jim Welsh, a freelance cameraman, and I met through a shared interest in filming and archiving the story of the east coast of Scotland's salmon netsmen whose industry faces difficulties and threats to its future. We produced a half-hour long DVD titled 'Silver Salmon and the Mechanical Pony', which includes scenes of the netsmen emptying their nets on St Cyrus beach. The film won a Golden Smokie award for Best Local Film at Arbroath's Fairport Film Festival in 2005.

The salmon-netting industry is heavily regulated by legislation. By law, the salmon nets must be 'slapped' or rendered ineffective to trap salmon over the period of the weekend. The jumper nets, which are anchored between the high and low water marks on the beach, are slapped by removing the 'leader'. This is an apron of net which hangs in the water, suspended on floats, between the shore and the back of the catching chamber. The migrating salmon, swimming along the shoreline, are guided by the leader into the catching chamber where they are trapped. When the leader is removed for the weekend the fish have free passage. Netting 'doors' can also be untied at the back of the net to allow any wayward salmon that still manage to get into the catching chamber to make their escape.

The salmon fishing industry's roots go back hundreds of years and, not surprisingly, it has built up its own distinctive vocabulary of words and phrases. The long-handled landing net which the fishermen use to remove the salmon from the nets is called a 'scum' net.

Summer

June - Miscellany

Whatever happened to fly cemeteries, those delicious, gooey, raisin-filled, buttery-pastry-top-and-bottom, sugary, cholesterol sins?

'I'll have one of those,' I said, pointing to one under the glass counter in a roadside restaurant.

'A fruit square?' asked the young lassie helpfully, looking at the grey hairs.

It was no use remonstrating. She would never have understood what I was talking about. I might have upset her and you can't do that sort of thing when you're a grandfather. Anyway, it was a fly rectangle.

Who first cooked up the description 'fly cemetery'? With a little imagination, it does look as though squashed flies, rather than sweet raisins, are what's sandwiched in these tasty pastries.

Driving past Inverkeilor, the fields were filled with buttercups. They say that, if someone holds a buttercup under your chin and the yellow petals reflect off your skin, you must like butter. If granddaughter Cecily had been with me, I could have held one under her chin and discussed her preferences with her.

Alternatively, we could have picked dandelion clocks and played 'He/she loves me, he/she loves me not' as we blew off the parachute seeds. A chancy business, mind you, as you need to take care you each get the right number of puffs to ensure that love is equal. With dandelion clocks, it's always best to finish on 'she loves me' or risk disappointment!

Do children still know about these harmless old-fashioned entertainments? You hardly ever see them playing such innocent games nowadays. Perhaps it's time for their revival.

A tit or a finch, I'm not sure which, flew straight off down the road in front of the car. By the time it got up to full speed it was doing about twenty-three miles an hour. It's quite staggering that such a small creature has so much power in its tiny frame. If we humans could convert our body weight into similar energy, we'd conquer the world.

Two early morning (about 5 a.m.) visitors to the bird table have been a red squirrel which comes for the peanuts and the woodpecker whose return is very welcome. Readers from the very start of this diary will remember the squirrel which featured in my first article. The woodpecker was also attracted by the nuts but didn't stay long. They are both such shy animals and probably prefer to come into the garden only when the dogs are indoors. Early as it was on each occasion, it was a great delight to see them both.

Despite these two visitors, the bird table is generally much less in demand from the rest of our resident birds. No doubt the supply of beetles, bugs and creepy-crawlies produced by the warmth of the early summer weather makes a very acceptable change of diet.

A shower of rain just as dusk was fading delayed my final outing with the dogs. In the damp, windless evening air, the smell of honeysuckle was overpowering. For me, it is the most romantic scent I know.

Due to illness, two old buddies who had missed each other for several days met up again in the village Post Office. 'It was my nerves, you see,' explained the patient. 'But I'm on the right road now. The doctor put me on a course o' thae tantalisers.'

It's a true story – the old lady needed tranquillisers to help settle her nerves.

July – Elderflower Cordial

I'm drinking a glass of the first of the Doyenne's delicious homemade elderflower cordial. This is living off nature's bounty. It's this year's first free offering from the countryside and we have it on our doorstep. Enormous soup-plate sized heads of elderflower blossom, ivory coloured and heavily scented, were cut from their bushes but that's where the free bit ends. Dissolve sugar and citric acid in boiling water and add lemon zest and slices. Trim the elderflower florets from the main stems and add to the 'bree'. Leave overnight and the next day strain into clean bottles. Couldn't be simpler but you have to remember it's a concentrate and must be diluted. Taken neat it will probably loosen your fillings!

It's a great lifesaver in the summertime. After an afternoon's heavy exertion cutting grass, nothing compares with the cool refreshing pleasure of a pint of cordial, served with loads of ice and a bunch of crushed mint leaves (preferably spearmint) scattered on top. Providentially, it can be frozen, prolonging the pleasure into autumn. And then there's the anticipation of the following summer when the whole mouth-watering process starts again.

I found a dead ferret by the roadside, which is unusual. Its coat wasn't the old ivory colour I'm used to but it had an almost brindled look – it may have been a cross with a polecat. The Doyenne saw another one, very similar, crossing the road near the gates of House of Dun, the National Trust property between Montrose and Brechin. I was told never to admit it if your ferret escapes. You should always deny it – say it has died and you forget where you buried it. An escaped ferret can do terrible damage if it gets into a henhouse at night – hence the need to distance yourself from any recriminations.

Swallows have built a nest under the eaves of the porch and they explode out of it every time we open the front door. I haven't disturbed them further by trying to look into it but I think the eggs should be close to hatching. We'll soon see small faces peering at us over the edge, waiting for the next treat of daddy-long-legs and other tasty insects.

Wild roses – or dog roses, as they are also called – are in flower everywhere. They are so attractive but die quickly if they are cut and put in a vase. The flowers grow in white and varying shades of pink though once, on a back road to Crieff, I came across a yellow one. Dog roses? It's hard to associate a hideous hound like Macbeth with such a delicate bush.

Sticky willy, the climbing weed whose round, dry seed pods stick to anything they catch on, is flourishing in the beech hedges. It was only several days ago, walking the dogs, when the early morning sun was shining on it that I realised it has tiny, white, four-pointed, star-shaped flowers.

From the Doyenne's Kitchen

Hedgerow Goodies

There's something very satisfying about food for free and being able to take advantage of the things growing around us and transform them into something delicious. Our regulars are brambles, rowans, elderflowers, field mushrooms and chanterelles and wild raspberries and strawberries

Here is my recipe for elderflower cordial.

ELDERFLOWER CORDIAL

20–25 large heads of elderflower
80 g citric acid
1 kg sugar
2 lemons

Method

Shake the elderflowers free of insects. Put the sugar in a large bowl and pour on 1.2 litres (2 pints) boiling water. Add the citric acid and mix well to dissolve. Grate in the zest of the 2 lemons then slice the lemons and add them. Put in the elderflowers, pressing them well down. Cover and leave overnight. Pour the liquid through a sieve and then through a jelly bag or muslin to clarify it. Put it into bottles and close tightly.

To serve as a drink, dilute with water or fizzy water and add ice and a slice of lemon. The syrup can also be added to fruit salads, gooseberry dishes and to ices. It doesn't have a long shelf life so I put mine into plastic tonic or mineral water bottles and keep them in the freezer.

Citric acid can be quite difficult to get these days. Some pharmacies sell it but, otherwise, you may need to find a shop that sells wine- and beer-making ingredients.

Early August - Midlothian Expedition

Tantallon Castle, just south of North Berwick, has to be one of the most exciting old castles to visit. Unoccupied for more than three hundred and fifty years, much of it is still complete and it hasn't been too badly plundered for its stones and masonry. It has been well restored by Historic Scotland and is an adventurous place to take youngsters like our four-year-old grandson Alfie.

The castle perches right on the edge of a cliff and looks out to the Bass Rock which is probably the best known nesting site for gannets in Britain. Covered in droppings from generations of the birds, it has a dirty yellow appearance. French POWs from the Napoleonic War were imprisoned on there and the conditions must have been more than usually harsh for them.

Tantallon was built in rose-red sandstone by the Douglas Earls of Angus. You can climb to the topmost parts of the castle ramparts to get exceptional views south to the Lammermuir Hills. Looking east over the River Forth and past the Bass, is the Isle of May, which is another important breeding site for seabirds.

Grass banks beside the pathways round the castle have been left to grow wild. We saw large numbers of green-veined white butterflies, which are common in this part of East Lothian. Above us, skylarks filled the air with their characteristic soaring song-flight.

Looking down from the high ramparts we had the unusual experience of watching house martins, easily recognisable by their white rump feathers, flying below us. Some were obviously nesting in the castle. Cormorants were clustered on rocks, standing with their wings akimbo, drying out their feathers. The sea was flat calm and, in spite of the rather overcast day, it was deep turquoise where the seaweed growing on the rocks stopped and the sand started.

We had a picnic down on the rocky beach and son James took his own son Alfie paddling in the rock pools. Hermit crabs had taken up residence in empty buckie shells and were crawling aggressively about the sandy bottom of the pools. Sandhoppers were hopping amongst the seaweed and the picnic was plagued with dozens of tiny flies.

A party of eider duck swam with the incoming tide into one of the bays, practically up to where we stood. Perhaps they were used to being fed by other picnickers – in which case, we were a disappointment to them. About fifty yards offshore, a seal popped its head through the calm surface of the sea and gazed at us odd humans scampering about the shore.

It was a great day out to share with our grandson and it was just as well Alfie took his sword with him to the castle to see off all the baddies!

Late August - Wildlife in the Workplace

Maternal protection of the young seems to be an instinct shared by the animal kingdom and us humans alike. I had a perfect example of it recently when the dogs and I were out for the evening walk.

We often turn off the road on to a farm track that leads down to a big field and looks across to the hills. It's not a long track – maybe fifty yards – and there is a central grassy strip between the two tractor wheel tracks. On this occasion, we had been very quiet coming along the road before turning sharply down the wee lane.

The dogs had run ahead of me and I was suddenly aware of a hen pheasant crouched in the grassy strip. There wasn't much cover and it sat absolutely motionless. I felt it was following my every move even though its eyes didn't blink. The dogs had passed it without seeing or scenting it.

My first thought was that it was injured – perhaps having been hit by a passing car. I bent down to look at it more carefully. The dogs realised I had stopped and came back to investigate. It was only when I stretched out my hand and with the caperings of the dogs as well that the poor bird lost her nerve and exploded into flight. As she rose, three chicks, cheepers just a day or so out of the nest, scattered in every direction, instinctively causing confusion. My main concern was for the survival of the chicks and to stop the dogs catching them. After this example of courage from the mother, they were all entitled to a more secure future. Once the panic subsided, she would have returned and collected her brood.

It was really quite late for a second hatching. I was surprised neither dog had picked up their scent because they passed within about a foot of the birds. It seems to bear out what I have heard – that some ground-nesting birds can suppress their scent during the nesting season.

I made a call to Sturrocks, the joiners at Whigstreet, just south of Forfar. I parked beside a large bush of white buddleia which was quivering with butterflies. Red admirals I could recognise but there were two or three other varieties clouding the bush – more than I have seen for quite some time. The explanation was inside the office. As a contribution to our environment, Sturrocks have created a low maintenance wildlife garden and planted it out with lavender, evergreens, herbaceous shrubs and hot-colour flowers. It's a wildlife haven sitting alongside all the busy industrial activity going on in their workshop. It's attracting numbers of butterflies, moths, grasshoppers, bees, birds and small mammals.

Now, isn't that a great idea that could be taken up by other businesses to bring colour and interest to their workplaces? It would give so much pleasure to their staff and to visitors.

Autumn

Early September - In the Midst of Life . . .

White pheasants, in my experience, are even more uncommon than white blackbirds. I saw maybe my fourth such mutant this past week. It was a young cock pheasant and he's completely white except for the scarlet wattles on his cheeks. He was running about the roadside – luckily, it was a back road that's well away from the heavy traffic. If he doesn't learn his kerb drill fast, he'll be no sort of pheasant at all very shortly.

Thrushes have been absent from the garden for many weeks. A wise friend has suggested that they depend for much of their feeding on earthworms and, as the ground has been so parched from lack of moisture, the worms have burrowed too far below the surface for the birds to reach them.

The recent rain may have been enough to bring the worms nearer the surface because several of the birds have been back to visit us. The ripening elderberries may also be tempting them. One in particular, a mistle thrush with a spectacular speckledy breast, has been catching my eye. He – or perhaps it is she – parades around the garden for all the world like a Brigade of Guards drill sergeant.

I watched the leaves cascading off a beech tree like a peaty stream. With the prolonged dry weather, many trees have suffered from lack of moisture and the slightest breeze is all that's needed to loosen their foliage. It's very inconsistent because others are still green and seem to be thriving. Our Scottish fall, much like the American fall when Americans go 'leaf peeping', is going to be early this year and may be pretty short-lived. It'll be part of the price of such a long, hot summer.

Rowans, too, have suffered from the dry spell. Most of the berries shrivelled on the branches before ripening and I had to scour the countryside to get enough for the Doyenne to make rowan and apple jelly, the best accompaniment ever for roast lamb.

By comparison, the brambles have flourished in the good weather and they are well formed and juicy. Pick out the fattest and ripest and have them with ice cream or mix them with your breakfast cereal – that's a great way to kick-start your taste buds. Brambling usually means hands and arms covered in scratches and nettle stings but the discomfort is a small price when the berries are as good as this year's.

A tiny, forlorn shrew sat on the stone step, with its back to the door, shaking with some terminal sickness. It never stirred when I opened the door and sat on the step to look at it. I picked it up and it sat feather-light in my palm, still trembling. Only when I put it down did it make a half-hearted attempt to take cover under a leaf. I expect nature will have taken its course by now.

Late September - The Broch

Barley stubbles, butter-yellow when freshly cut, soon turned to faded sun-bleach during the endless days of sunshine we enjoyed over the summer. Now, after a night's heavy rain, they look as lifeless as they are. Already the ploughs have been into the fields, turning under the dead stalks and exposing the brown sheen of next season's tilth ready for sowing.

Oilseed rape is the first crop to be sown for next year's harvest. No sooner were this year's bales of straw carted out of the fields than some were ploughed up. The rape was sown straight after and already it is far enough through to produce a green carpet of colour. It won't grow much more over winter but, in springtime, the ground-high shoots will sprout at a great pace to a height of about five feet – ready for the eternal round of harvesting once more.

The weather has turned really back end-ish all of a sudden. There's a chill in the air and my fair-weather dogs are not so keen to spend their days outside.

I welcome the calls of the returning geese but I don't look forward to the shortening days.

We've planned another visit to son Robert and his family but this time to the Banffshire coast where they are holidaying. We joined them at Portknockie which is one of the fishing villages strung along that north-facing coast from Fraserburgh westwards to the Moray Firth. Peter F. Anson describes the village in *Fishing Boats and Fisher Folk on the East Coast of Scotland*. He wrote that Portknockie was one of the most flourishing fishing centres on the Moray Firth in the 1930s. Even when its harbour had been enlarged, it could not hold the fleet of fifty-eight steam drifters which belonged to the 555 fishermen 'of this very much alive little place'.

The whole coastline was, at one time, greatly dependent on the herring and white fishing for a livelihood. Each village has its harbour and, as I am unable to pass any harbour without going down to have a look, I had a deeply fulfilling weekend.

Walking the dogs, we disturbed a handsome buck hare, which cantered away from us quite unconcerned. He well knew he was in no danger from Sheba's old legs or Macbeth's short ones but the company wasn't to his liking. I'm always pleased to see a hare and always optimistic they'll return to their former numbers once more.

Macbeth was taking no chances on getting home again. We woke up on the Sunday morning to find he had settled himself very cosily into the overnight bag we had brought our kit in. If you're a dog with as much in the brains department as a docken, I suppose it's obvious what an overnight bag is for.

Granddaughter Cecily announced she would sit opposite me at breakfast, explaining that 'then I can gaze into your eyes'. Game, set and match to Cecily!

Early November - Countryside Musings

Glen Prosen was my destination last Saturday. It was a favourite place of my father who was born and brought up in Kirriemuir. As a youngster, he used to cycle to the glen and scramble about its braes. Bikes were heavy machines in those days and they were often referred to as 'pushbikes'. It must have taken a lot of push and puff to slog his way up the hills from Kirrie.

I was bowling round a corner and had to brake to avoid a pheasant crossing the road. I was concentrating so much on the bird I nearly didn't notice the wildcat that was sneaking back into the undergrowth on the opposite verge. So perhaps that was one lucky pheasant and one hungry wildcat swicked out of its breakfast!

The Clan Macpherson crest is a Scottish wildcat and their motto is 'Touch not the cat bot a glove', meaning don't touch the cat without the protection of a glove – the inference being that a Macpherson warrior was, and possibly still is, as unpredictable and ferocious as a wildcat with its claws unsheathed.

Hopefully, the recent rain has raised the level of the Prosen Water enough to let the salmon up to their spawning grounds. A clip on the TV news showed fish in the River Ericht being netted and helped over the weir at Blairgowrie. So, while it's been great suntan weather for us humans, there may be an ecological account to be paid for in future years.

On my way back down the glen I passed a melanistic cock pheasant, something I haven't seen for several seasons. I understand they are not hybrid birds but that they have an abnormally high level of black pigment in their feathers. This gives them a dark, burnished sheen, similar to a starling's colouring, making them particularly handsome birds.

Near the foot of the glen is a memorial to Captain Scott of the Antarctic and Dr Edward Wilson who died with him. Capt. Scott planned his last fateful trip to the South Pole in a bungalow close by the cairn which belonged to the Wilson family. Dundee and Montrose readers who are getting smoother in the tooth will remember Largs music shops. Mr Eric Larg and his sister lived in that same bungalow for some years.

My father told me that my grandfather, who was a partner in Wilkie & Dundas Solicitors in Kirriemuir, knew Capt. Scott. Father handed on a banjo to me. He said Scott had left the instrument in my grandfather's care. It has pen-and-ink cartoons of dancing figures on its skin and they were supposed to have been drawn by Edward Wilson. Wilson was a fine artist but the dancers on the banjo are quite crude, especially when compared to the reproductions of his delicate work that appear in his biography. Nevertheless, I like to believe the story is true for why would my grandfather invent a story like that?

Now the mystery of the story of the banjo has deepened. Amongst my father's papers, I have subsequently found a photograph (date unknown) of my grandfather David Whitson and his friend Edward Young, son of Lord Young, a Lord of the Court of Session. In the photo, the pair are sitting at a small table in a garden. It is evident from the opened bottles that they are having a thoroughly convivial time and one – or perhaps both – has been playing the banjo which rests against the table. Father has written on the back – 'Banjo was at the Antarctic with Wilson who did some sketches on the parchment of mice, cow jumping over the moon, etc.'

If the banjo in the photograph is the same as the one in my possession, the photo was taken before it went to the Antarctic because there are no cartoons on the skin. The conundrum, therefore, is how did the banjo get into Captain Scott's possession, as told by my father? Or was it lent to Dr Wilson? Was it Edward Wilson who drew the cartoons? And, if, indeed, it went to the Antarctic, how did it make its way back to Kirriemuir and my grandfather?

There is another strand to the story. My great uncle, Sir Toby Whitson (David Whitson's brother), was an Edinburgh chartered accountant. He was friendly with the polar explorer and oceanographer William Speirs Bruce who led the Scottish National Antarctic Expedition 1902–1904. This expedition was overshadowed by

Captain Scott's 1901–1904 'furthest south' expedition, which brought him acclaim as a national hero. I have a photograph of Bruce and his ship's officers, including Uncle Toby, who is noted as 'Hon Accountant'. So, is this the polar connection? Obviously there is more research that can be done.

Late November - Saint and the Cheese

To Hexham again but this time on grandparenting duty so that son Robert and his wife Katie can travel to Munster, in Germany, where Robert's regiment is stationed. Four days without their parents might have been a bit alarming for granddaughter Cecily and grandson Fergus but it was no less daunting for the Doyenne and me. Anyhow, it all passed off brilliantly, except perhaps for old Sheba who patiently endured two-year-old Fergus hurling himself in enthusiastic affection onto her sore old bones.

Hexham has a racecourse and there are racehorses in the fields beside the house. Macbeth was fascinated by such immense 'dogs' and braced his nerves to creep up to the fences and touch noses with some of them. He turned tail pretty quickly when they blew down their noses at him and he scampered back to me, only at the last moment swaggering up as if to say, 'Just checking things out.'

The next-door dog is called Hamish and it reassured Macbeth to have another apparent Scot on his side. Hamish's owner tells me he – Hamish, that is – is a Manchester terrier which is a breed I hadn't come across. He looks like a spring-loaded black-and-tan version of a Jack Russell.

On the way home, we stopped at Turvelaws Farm beside Wooler where we were entertained on leek and tattie soup (the husband is a tattie grower) and some equally appetising Cuddy's Cave cheese. The name derives from St Cuthbert who made a pilgrimage from Melrose to Lindisfarne and spent a night in a cave near the farm. It's a delicious, locally-made mild cheese and I asked our hostess where I could buy some to take home. She directed me to two very helpful cheesemongering ladies in The Good Life Shop and also suggested their Northumbrian nettle cheese which she thought we would enjoy. Too right – they were both most tasty and, as recommended by the cheesemongering ladies, much improved with a glass of good red wine.

'Turve' apparently is north country for soil. And 'law', in this instance, I suspect is likely to mean low place, as the farm lies in a valley. So the name could be a reference to a low-lying fertile place, which is good news if you're growing tatties.

We drove south on the A68 and back on the A697 which is a road we haven't used for a while. You're still driving through the grand Border countryside but we'd forgotten just how quiet this road is. Not that the A68 is particularly busy either. Northumberland is the least populated English county and this is very evident when travelling on these relatively car-free roads.

Sheba actually looked visibly relieved to be home again, to the familiar places and smells. After four non-stop days on duty, the Doyenne and I were visibly relieved to get home too!

From the Doyenne's Kitchen

Finding enough entertainment to keep two active grandchildren entertained for four days fairly stretched my creativity. Luckily, cooking can always be counted on to help keep little minds and hands busy.

CHOCOLATE CAKE

This is my mother's chocolate cake recipe which made many a birthday cake for our children. It has now become the traditional birthday cake for the grandchildren. What *really* makes it is the chocolate fudge icing which is a recipe given to me by my sister-in-law. It's so good there's always a fight to clean out the pan.

For the cake:
4 oz butter
4 oz sugar

4 oz self-raising flour
2 eggs, beaten
salt
2oz drinking chocolate powder

For the chocolate fudge icing:
2½ oz margarine
4 tbsp cocoa or drinking chocolate powder
8 oz sieved icing sugar
3 tbsp scalded milk
1 tsp vanilla essence

Method

Cream the butter and sugar. Add the beaten eggs and flour and a pinch of salt. Put the drinking chocolate powder in a bowl and mix with hot water to a thin paste. Add to the mixture and mix in well.

Pour the mixture into an 8" round, greased cake tin and cook at 180°C for 30 minutes or until firm. Turn out and leave to cool.

Meanwhile, make the chocolate fudge icing by melting margarine, together with the cocoa or drinking chocolate – I use 2 tbsp of both. Remove from the heat. Stir in icing sugar, milk and vanilla essence and beat until thick.

Split the cooled cake in half horizontally and sandwich the top and bottom pieces together with the chocolate fudge icing, dribbling the remainder over the top.

AUNTIE WIN BISCUITS

Auntie Win was a great chum of my mother. Her father was Governor General of Australia and her husband owned the company that made Kamella baby bags – if anyone remembers those! I remember her as a large and wise lady, much respected by us all. She always had a biscuit tin full of these delicious crispy biscuits when we went to visit. They are so easy to make, the mixture makes loads and they are very grandchildren-friendly.

5 oz Trex (a vegetarian alternative to lard)
2 tablespoons syrup
4 oz porridge oats
4 oz sugar
5 oz plain flour
1 tsp baking powder
1 tsp bicarbonate of soda
a little milk

Method

Melt the Trex and syrup in a pan. Remove from the heat.

Put the oats, sugar and flour in a bowl and pour over the melted Trex and syrup. Mix the baking powder and bicarbonate of soda together in a cup with the milk. This will bubble and fizz – but it's meant to. Add it to the mixture and stir really well. Grease baking sheets. Roll teaspoonfuls of mixture into balls and place them on the baking sheets.

Cook in a hot oven for about 10 minutes or until biscuits are golden brown. Take the baking sheets out of the oven and leave the biscuits to set for a minute or so. Remove from baking tray with a palette knife and put them on a wire cooling rack. Allow the biscuits to cool completely and then store them in an airtight tin.

2003 – 2004

Winter

December - Cows May Fly

Macbeth is closer to nature than Sheba. It's most apparent at this time of year when we get home from walks and he trails half the countryside indoors with him hanging from his stomach. He's not due his next clip until mid-January but the closer it gets to barber time, the more he looks like a rather earnest version of Paw Broon, the cartoon character who appears each week in *The Sunday Post*.

Like Paw Broon, it's wise to keep a warm bunnet handy during the unpredictable weather. Apparently 40% of the body's heat goes straight out the top of our heads so it's best to trap it before it contributes to global warming!

It's the time also to keep bird tables well stocked with food. It's effort that repays itself in the continued pleasure you will get from the garden songbirds.

We've made some changes to Sheba's diet and the vet has given her a different heart pill. She seems to be ending the year in rather better trim than she started. It's not made her any less thrawn when she's so inclined – or when she's disinclined is perhaps more the point. But we certainly see an improvement in her energy.

Last Monday, the twenty-second, was the shortest day. By half past three, it was dusk and, by half past four, quite dark. I'm quite excited by the prospect that, from now on, the days will lengthen as spring gets closer. Stubble fields where we have walked the dogs are ploughed up now. This is inevitable if next year's crops are to be sown on time. So it's back into the woods again for walking where we get some shelter from winter winds.

The Doyenne and I went to a service of carols and readings which was organised to support a charity called Send a Cow. This is a charity which encourages self-help amongst the poorest members of the poorest communities in East Africa by sending them livestock – cows, goats, pigs, bees and poultry. Assisting sustainable agriculture in this way meets the needs, in a very direct manner, of those who benefit, by helping them produce milk and meat for improved nutrition and increase soil fertility and crop production.

The congregation fairly raised the roof with a lot of joyful carols. The timing of the service and the name of the charity were most apposite – what could be more fitting than 'the cattle are lowing, the baby awakes' from 'Away in a Manger'?

And the good news to end the year with is that enough was collected to ensure that a cow will soon be on its way to help sustain a poor family in a far-off place. Hard to think of a better practical demonstration of Christmas generosity.

Early January – Down by the Riverside

Last Saturday, the first of the New Year, the Doyenne and I took the dogs off down the bank of the River North Esk to where the river finally meets with the sea. We'd just entertained son Robert, his wife Katie and their lively young family to a quick and rowdy lunch. It was time for some peace!

The sea is a relentless beast. We climbed over the dunes that protect the land from the tides and stood for a while on the sand just watching the waves break unceasingly on the beach. The mid-afternoon sun was getting low in the west and we cast enormous shadows.

To the south, at the end of Montrose Bay, Scurdie Ness Lighthouse was blinking its message of comfort to mariners. Looking northwards up the coast the tall spire of St Cyrus Church rises prominently above the cliffs that the village is built on. It must have been a reassuring daytime aid to navigation for generations of sailors and fishermen and probably still is despite modern satellite systems.

We turned back up the riverbank again. Flotsam and jetsam are strewn all around the river mouth, thrown up on the banks by the high winter tides.

Several small packs of geese flew in to feed on stubbles at Waterside Farm on the far side of the river. In the Fluke Hole, a large pool eroded into the riverbank, two swans were elegantly passing the time of day. Curlews with their curving, probing beaks, were feeding in a grass field. 'Whaups' was the traditional Scottish name my father always used for these birds and they have an evocative, melancholy cry that conjures up the open, windswept places where they are often seen.

The river runs a lot faster than it seems. It is tidal by now and there are few shallows to break up the surface of the water, which has a deep and uninterrupted flow in its last fling before it meets the sea. Soon the spring run of salmon will be heading upriver to spawn.

There were only two other families on the beach – both walking their dogs like us. We are so lucky to have such marvellous beaches at Montrose and St Cyrus to walk dogs on. Perhaps they are undervalued but they are certainly underused – although it was great to have the privacy of all that sand and sea to ourselves.

Macbeth nearly blew a gasket sniffing all the absorbing smells he found in the gorse clumps along the riverside. Old Sheba had been there before, seen it all and even had the hair shirt! 'If age but could and youth but knew,' she seemed to say, as she just kept hirpling (limping) along the track.

As we reached the car, the smell of peat smoke drifted from one of the cottages. Now, that's quite unusual in this part of the world.

Late January – Wooden House

First snowdrop of the season goes to a neighbour who tells me her first flower appeared on Christmas Day. I had a look round our own garden but not a sign of one – although one crocus (I think, I'm not very clever on bulbs) has poked its green nose through and there are a couple of cheery yellow primulas providing a wee flash of colour.

In a *Book of Days*, I read that the snowdrop is January's flower and February is associated with the violet, which seems a little out of place in a Scottish winter. I can well imagine any violet wanting to shrink from some of the coarse weather February throws at us.

I decided to take the Forfar–Coupar Angus road on a recent trip to Perth and, as I passed a wall of tattie boxes built beside the road at Castleton of Eassie, I remembered a story I heard about twenty years ago. The potato merchant who had his business there was inspecting his boxes at the start of a new season and found one with the end knocked out. A tramp had roofed and lined the box with polythene bags and turned it into his winter home. I suppose for someone who chooses that sort of life it was a pretty sensible place to pitch camp. With all the improvements it would have been windproof, waterproof, bijou and private – and it had the social kudos of a country address!

The Doyenne reported seeing a stoat in ermine near the gates of House of Dun, between Montrose and Brechin. Winter snows trigger a change from the stoats' reddish-brown summer colouring to a pure white winter camouflage. But the black tip of the tail gets forgotten in the metamorphosis and always stays black.

With climate change, we've experienced much milder weather in recent winters and a lot less snow falling. If that's to be the pattern for future years, the stoat's wintertime transformation may cease to be relevant. The white ermine trimmings on the ceremonial robes of their lordships of the House of Lords are from the winter coat of the stoat. In view of the proposed changes to reform the House of Lords, stoats in ermine may have to live on borrowed time for only a short time longer.

In Montrose Museum, an exhibition of watercolours by Montrose artist William Lamb, who died in 1951, has opened. Many are views painted locally and record fishermen and local people at work. There is an articulation and natural freedom expressed through the local subjects that could only have come from knowing and living with the people and places. For me and, I'm sure, many other Montrosians old enough to remember, they recall what hard physical work the inshore and salmon fishing was.

February - Self-Sufficiency

Fresh bread, baked this morning, and this year's home-made marmalade – both made by the Doyenne, of course – are the ingredients of the dream breakfast. But, if you had visions of the Doyenne up to her oxters in dough, I have to set the record straight. Son Robert and his family gave us a bread-making machine for Christmas. Everything happens in the baking pan overnight and, when the pinger goes in the morning, the house fills with the wonderful smell of that day's loaf.

As soon the Seville oranges appeared in the shops, La D. has her mother's jelly pan on the cooker. She uses a marmalade recipe given her by another Yorkshire girl, Mrs Ann Keddie, so she feels confident about its provenance. The generous shadow that I cast is testimony to how good the bread and marmalade breakfasts are.

I was roused from my lazy Saturday morning by a tremendous thrumming noise and dashed outside. Three helicopters were flying north-east, in line astern, in an absolutely flawless ice-blue sky. I would have loved to be up there with them for the views must have been endless.

There was a coorse wind last Sunday morning and the dogs and I stood just inside the wood, getting what shelter we could from a broad sycamore tree. The wind chased the snow in squalls across the face of the Caterthuns (one Brown and the other White), the two hills topped with Pictish Iron Age forts of the same name, which, in summer, make such good family walks. Each snow shower passed like pages turning in a book. We watched each gust starting somewhere about Fordoun and scampering across the brae faces, as they were whipped along by the wind. Momentarily the hills were obliterated and then they appeared again, just as fleetingly, before the next dose of snow went flinging past on its way to Kirriemuir.

As I started the car to unfreeze the windscreen, I noticed the red squirrel feeding on the peanuts. The Doyenne came out and, while we chatted noisily to each other, the squirrel just carried on feeding. I got to within about six feet of him – or perhaps it was her – before it lost its nerve and reluctantly dropped to the ground and dashed to the tall spruce tree.

Since I started writing these weekly pieces, it's been most instructive to get so much closer to the animals and birds that I saw quite regularly in the past and just took for granted. I can't ever do that again now.

It's interesting too to note the changes that take place over a year. This time last year, there were mallard duck all around. Some evenings the pond across the field had up to two dozen birds chattering away to each other and calling greetings to passing chums. This year the pond has been practically abandoned and it's only now that a small pack of four are dropping into a pool in the burn beside the house, with any regularity.

From the Doyenne's Kitchen

Jams and jellies are an important part of the yearly cycle and one of the most important preserves in my store cupboard is marmalade. Sharp, chunky, golden marmalade made with Seville oranges on toast or fresh bread – there's nothing like it.

This recipe was given to me by a dear Yorkshire friend. Making it is a labour of love and every minute of the time spent is worth it as it's the best marmalade I've ever tasted. I spread the making of it over about three days, doing a stage at a time.

Seville oranges are only in the shops for a short time in January so you do have to keep an eye open for them as they go quickly. They freeze well if you don't have time to make your marmalade when they are fresh.

ANN'S MARMALADE

3 sweet oranges
4 small or 3 large lemons
enough Seville oranges to take the total weight of fruit to 4 lbs
10 pints water
10 lbs preserving sugar

Method

There's a lot in this recipe and you could make two lots from the beginning or boil it in two batches when you get to the last stage. I do it all in one but I am fortunate to have a large china mixing bowl and my mother's big brass preserving pan.

Wipe the fruit, halve it and squeeze the juice into a bowl. Take the pips and wrap them in muslin. Put the halves of the fruit, the pulp, the juice and the bag of pips into a large china bowl with the water and leave to soak overnight.

Next day, turn it all, including the bag of pips which I tie on to the handle, into a preserving pan. Bring slowly to the boil, then simmer the fruit until quite tender. Leave to cool, put back in the bowl and leave to stand another night.

Take out the skins and slice them very finely. Rub the inside of the preserving pan with butter and return the chopped skins and all the liquid to the pan and bring to the boil. Take the bag of pips out of the pan and let it cool on a plate. Then, by hand (my method), squeeze all the juice and pectin out of the pips on to a plate and pour the liquid back into the pan. Add the sugar and stir over a medium heat until the sugar has dissolved. Bring the liquid to a rapid boil and, after 30 minutes or so, test for a set.

To test for a set, put a small amount of the liquid on to a clean, cold saucer or plate and let it cool a little. Then draw your finger across it and, if the liquid crinkles, you have a set. If not, boil for another 5 to 10 minutes and try again.

Spring

March - Strange Tongues

A solitary tree pokes its silhouette above the skyline of a hill in the distance. It is the only tree that stands beside the path to the Brown Caterthun, one of two Iron Age forts lying to the north of Brechin, and the hilltop neighbour of White Caterthun. Every time we – the dogs and I, that is – take our walk in the woods, that tree catches my eye. It's a Scotch pine, I believe, and we shall take a walk to the old hill before much longer, just to check.

Talking of which, about a year ago, I mentioned 'Scotch pines' in my Saturday piece and was taken to task for not calling them 'Scots pines', which I was assured is their proper designation. My Loanhead auntie called them Scotch pines, and I should have liked to have seen my detractor telling *her* she was wrong. He wouldn't have got just a flea in his ear – he'd have got a wasps' byke around his head.

Talking of which – when I brought the Doyenne, as a bride of scarce one summer, to live at Logie Pert she used to drive an elderly neighbour, Jim Foreman, to Craigo Post Office every Monday to collect his pension. Jim had worked locally on farms all his life, almost entirely within the boundaries of the county of Angus. The Doyenne came from Bradford and was keen to integrate. I think they enjoyed racy conversations all the way to Craigo and back but neither understood a word the other was saying!

One Monday Jim warned her about 'twa bykes in the dyke'. To a Yorkshire lass, a 'byke' is a bicycle and a 'dyke' is a ditch. She was profoundly nonplussed about the significance of 'two bicycles in the ditch'. It took a little serious explanation to get her round that one! A translation of 'twa bykes in the dyke' may be helpful for other Yorkshire brides. 'Byke' is a wasp's nest and 'dyke' is a wall. Jim was warning the Doyenne to avoid the two wasps' nests which he had seen in the garden wall.

Several weeks ago, I mentioned Edzell Blue potatoes, an old-fashioned, blue-skinned, floury potato with superb taste, sadly now scarcely available. The old name for Edzell was Slateford but the even earlier name for the village was Aigle. Every year, Jim Foreman grew a few rows of Aigle Blues and he was the only person I have ever heard in a lifetime spent in Angus, refer to the village by its oldest name, as a habit of daily speech. As with so many of the traditional varieties, it is now quite hard to track down seed of these delicious potatoes – even for garden cultivation – but it's worth the effort to do so. A whole one (boiled, of course!) popped into a bowl of hare soup takes what is already a superb meal to a higher plane.

In the 1950s and '60s, my father sometimes took me to the Sauchieburn Inn, near Fettercairn. It was an interesting place and I heard the locals – farm workers, farmers, tradesmen and businessmen – using the old vernacular of the district in their regular conversation. Much of it now seems to have completely fallen from use, probably due to the influence of television.

Old Mrs Watson owned the pub and the bar was the old farmhouse kitchen where we sat round an enormous pine table. She served us from her wheelchair, pushing herself to and from the drink store in the back. There was no draught beer – just bottled, which I drank – and Father, as ever, drank drams.

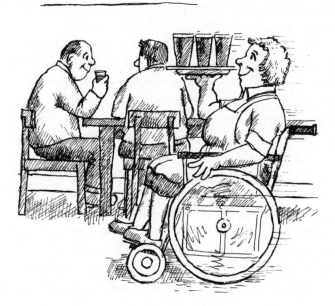

April - Historical Walks

The Doyenne can be pretty eagle-eyed at times – usually when it's least convenient for me! Lately, she was in the midst of a lengthy telephone conversation with a friend when she broke off to say, 'A wren has just flown out of the old swallows nest.'

I watched the nest for a couple of minutes and, sure enough, the wren returned with a beakful of moss and disappeared into the nest which swallows had built last year in the eaves of the porch. Both birds were busy bringing material to convert the big nest into a bijou residence for smaller lodgers. They have narrowed the entrance and lined the inside mostly with dry moss and grasses. It'll be interesting to see if the swallows return this year and start another nest next door.

I took my promised walk to the Brown Caterthun and by luck chose a lovely mild morning. The clouds were high and the sun warm and it just was great to be outdoors. The views from both the White and Brown Caterthun (which lie several miles north of Brechin) are stunning, and as neither is a hard walk they are ideal outings for small walkers.

Once I'd got to the top, I tried to get a fix on our house but as it is quite wooded round about I couldn't see it with the naked eye. However smoke from a neighbour's bonfire, which he was just starting as I left home, helped me pinpoint it. An enormous Wellingtonia towering above fir trees helped to locate Lundie Castle which lies at the foot of the Brown hill. I could just see the ridge of the roof and its flagpole, which was flying the Scottish saltire.

'Fleg' is a scarcely used Scots word for a fright and I got a right one when I all but trod on a grouse in the heather, which erupted like a rocket from under my feet. Easier on the nerves were the skylarks. One rose into the sky and hung there singing its heart out and that was the signal for half a dozen more to join in. I stood in the sunshine, hingin' over a gate, and listened. The poet Shelley wrote of their song as 'a rain of melody' and that's just how it was – I was showered with their tunes.

The Caterthuns were constructed up to 4500 years ago, so it's difficult to be precise about their purpose. I believe that, being so well sited geographically on the top of hills with tremendous fields of vision, there are, at least in part, military and defensive explanations for them.

Blue painted wee Scotchmen, without JCBs, picks or shovels, horses or wheels, built these impressive hill forts effectively with their bare hands. As they are several acres in size, they are extraordinary feats of human endeavour. Their builders must have understood more than just basic engineering skills and have had well-developed concepts of strategic planning.

Early May - Death of a Friend

Old Sheba is dead and, while we feel sadness at her loss, we are thankful that her discomfort and pain are ended.

Her heart sounded like a leaky washing machine and she was in constant pain from the arthritis in her legs but, right to the end, she wagged her tail in greeting to us and to the world at large.

Sheba came to us twelve years ago when she was two years old. We were told she had only ever spent half an hour inside a house so we anticipated her arrival with some trepidation. But, from the moment she walked through our door, she behaved with faultless good manners. She heartily endorsed the change from kennel life and repaid our confidence by her constant good behaviour and clean habits.

It's not wise to attribute human characteristics to one's pets but Sheba was the most considerate and kindly disposed dog I've ever encountered. She was certainly the best-trained dog I've owned. I can't claim the credit for her training but she never forgot it and I rarely needed to remind her. Out walking on country roads was never a problem. She returned to heel at the sound of a car and sat at the verge until it passed.

Not that she lacked character. She could be thrawn – to the extent that sharp words would pass. But she was always gracious in acceptance of such setbacks and would come back, tail wagging, looking for a tickle.

Grandchildren jumped on her and crawled over her and she took it all in good humour. She'd had one litter of puppies before I bought her and I would have liked to have continued her line but she had to have a hysterectomy which put paid to the idea.

Sheba enjoyed visiting and we confidently took her with us to Edinburgh flats and country houses alike. When it was time to leave she was always first to be included in the invitation to come again!

When she couldn't accompany us we were fortunate to have very friendly kennelling on a farm close to home. We dropped her off and she went into her kennel without a backward glance. She accompanied the farmer around the farm without any need of a lead. She just enjoyed the familiarity of human contact.

As the arthritis grew worse, her limp became more pronounced. She took it all without complaint. The most I heard was a grunt of protest (never any ill will) when the vet had to manipulate her joints to see just how bad her symptoms were.

She's buried in a corner of a wood where we often walked, beside fields she roamed over, and with a glimpse of hills she frequently looked to – all very familiar.

In unsentimental terms, Sheba was put down because her state of health was such that keeping her alive was doing so only for her to get worse. The final decision was mine and was taken because, in my view, her quality of life had deteriorated to the point where living was insupportable.

Sentimental as this poem is, it says something of what I thought when I took her to the vet and afterwards.

If It Should Be

If it should be that I grow frail and weak
And pain should keep me from my sleep,
Then you must do what must be done
For this last battle can't be won.
You will be sad, I understand.
Don't let your grief then stay your hand
For this day more than all the rest
Your love and friendship stand the test.
We've had so many happy years
What is to come can hold no fears.
You won't let me suffer, that I know,
When time is up, please let me go.
Take me where my needs they'll tend
And just stay with me to the end,
And hold me firm and speak to me
Until my eyes no longer see.
In time it will be clear to you
It is a kindness that you do.
Although my tail its last has waved
From pain and suffering I've been saved.
And do not grieve it should be you
Who must decide this thing to do.
We've been so close these many years
Don't let your heart hold any tears.

Anon

She's laid by now and, to paraphrase a few words
from Shakespeare, for Sheba, the rest is silence.

Late May – Big Tree Country

Big tree country is what they call Perthshire and quite rightly so when you see the magnificent stands of trees planted by the Victorians at places like the Hermitage near Dunkeld and growing, apparently free seeded, in Glen Lyon and around Aberfoyle.

But 'bluebell country' would have been just as apt a description when the Doyenne and I drove through the county on our way to the west coast, to spend a few congenial days with congenial friends. The roadsides on the A984 between Coupar Angus and Dunkeld and then up the A9 to Pitlochry were just awash with brilliant patches of the flowers in amongst the trees and on the verges. The Doyenne, who was round that way on business, came across the Kinclaven bluebell wood and she told me the whole floor of the wood, as far as she could see, was just a solid carpet of blue. She had rarely seen so bonny a sight.

Mr Gordon Dilworth is a regular contributor to the Letters column of the *The Courier* and he also keeps a critical eye on my Saturday articles. He took me to task for my description of the roadside flowers as 'bluebells', having just, himself, written to the newspaper deploring the growing habit of erroneously applying the name to our native Scottish harebells.

Bluebells is the name commonly given in England (not Scotland) to wild blue hyacinths. By contrast, that iconic (made in Sweden now!) national product,

Scottish Bluebell matches, shows a picture of harebells on the box. So it's clear how easily confusion can arise from the most innocent remark. As ever, I cravenly sought refuge behind the skirts of my Loanhead auntie, writing to Mr Dilworth that my aunt 'differentiated between harebells as one very distinct Scottish wild flower and bluebells as another. Her bluebells are your wild hyacinths'.

Here's another conundrum. In springtime, I see pink and white wild hyacinths growing in the woods where we walk. Are they pinkbells and whitebells or have they free seeded from gardens? Anyway, for the record, the flowers the Doyenne and I saw driving on our trip to the West were definitely bluebells!

There's something very reassuring about going back to a place year after year and we always look forward to the familiarity of our annual visit to Kinlochewe and Loch Maree. That part of the Highlands still has lots of evidence of Victorian land management with handsome wellingtonias and Douglas firs and wild rhododendrons.

Last year, we discovered Attadale Gardens on Lochcarron-side and we went back again this year to properly explore what we think is the loveliest woodland garden we have visited in the Highlands. Although it predates the Victorians, the present layout was planted in the 1890s. As is so often the case with the best west-coast gardens, it lies in the shelter of steep cliffs and tall conifers, which is what makes it possible to grow so many almost tropical plants. Everything is so much in harmony with its surroundings and ponds and paths draw the eye into the landscape.

What a wonderful place for youngsters to grow up in. Tangles of hundred-year-old rhododendrons make secret gang hideouts and there is an old wood of giant sequoia redwoods and mature native trees which is a tranquil place to stop in.

And everywhere there was colour – early rowan blossom, copper-red maple trees, azaleas, tall candelabra primulas and every shade of green from native and imported flowers and foliage.

What an undertaking and what commitment – and how generous to share it all with others! There isn't the space to tell you everything but, if you find yourself in Wester Ross, take some time to visit Attadale yourself.

While we were away, Macbeth went to new kennels. As it was his first time away from home on his own, we were concerned that he might miss his old friend Sheba. We needn't have worried – when we collected him, it was clear he had captured all the girls' hearts and been thoroughly spoiled.

Summer

Early July - Man's Best Friend

Summer has some catching up to do. The summer solstice has passed, which means the longest day and shortest night are gone for another year. Midsummer's Day has been celebrated too so we should be enjoying warm sunny weather such as we had this time last year instead of the cold and rain we've had over recent days.

Last weekend, the Doyenne and I visited the garden of Newton Mill House, between Brechin and Edzell, which was open under the Scottish Gardens Scheme. We were close enough to walk there and we took Macbeth along with us. A notice at the gate said 'No Dogs' so I was preparing to walk Macbeth back home again but was told that as he is 'practically family' an exception could be made. The gift of neighbours!

It must be a nerve-racking business preparing to open one's garden to the public – the weather usually has the final say however cleverly one anticipates what it may do. Mrs Rose Rickman has developed her garden at Newton Mill for nearly twenty years now and there seems to be a near-perfect symmetry between Newton Mill House and its walled garden.

We were much impressed by the terrific show of roses and delphiniums and the outstanding herbaceous borders were packed with colour and lots more to come. The vegetables were immaculate too, everything standing to attention and neatly labelled. I noticed one row of potatoes marked Edzell Blues, not with their old name of 'Aigle Blues' as I wrote about several weeks back.

Forfar Carriage Driving Group, which is part of Riding for the Disabled Association, were to benefit from the proceeds of the day. The group has a horse-drawn carriage which is adapted to take a wheelchair so that people with all levels of disability can enjoy time in the countryside.

The intelligence and devotion of dogs was graphically demonstrated recently. A friend was walking his two Labradors by the side of a river when he slipped and tumbled over a high bank. Luckily some bushes broke his fall or he would have fallen on to rocks. He dislocated his shoulder and found himself unable to get back up the bank with only the one good arm.

The old dog sat at the top of the bank to look after his master and the young dog ran back along the path until it met two other walkers. The dog barked and capered in front of the walkers making it clear that it needed help. Thankfully the walkers weren't fazed by the dog's behaviour and followed it to where its master was still trying to extricate himself.

As his wife said, 'It's like something out of Lassie.' Lassie was a wonderful, film-star Border collie which spent its film career rescuing people from dangers and leading them to safety. But you have to be a certain age to remember all that!

As a postscript to this, here's what Mrs Beattie from Dunfermline wrote to me:

> Dear Mr Whitson
> I enjoyed your story 'Man with two dogs' on Saturday 3rd July – but I must disagree with you on one point – 'Lassie' was not a Border collie but a Rough collie. And did you know 'Lassie' was in fact a 'Laddie'! Keep the stories coming!

Her letter just showed me how important it is to check my facts before I leap into print!

Late July - Celtic Culture and Salmon Fishers

'Living history' regularly drew howls of despair from our children as we marched them into old churches, castles and other ancient piles. Promises of how much fun it was going to be fell on deaf ears!

Driving home from Forfar to Brechin on the Aberlemno road, which is such a favourite with its tremendous views up and down Strathmore, I had a spur-of-the-moment thought to visit Aberlemno Church and replenish the living history.

I wanted to look again at the eighth-century Celtic carved stone in the graveyard which has such a vivid battle scene on its back. Foot soldiers – kernes and gallowglasses, if you remember your Shakespeare – buckled and helmeted, with sword and targe. And their officers on horseback, armed with long lances. And the front is intricately decorated with a cross formed with flourishes of Celtic knots each without a beginning and without end.

The sculptor was probably quite uneducated because education was for the 'quality', unless you were in the church. But his eye for narrative and beauty didn't suffer from a lack of formal schooling. Weeks, possibly months, he would have spent chiselling the story of the battle on one side and, on the other, attributing victory to divine mediation.

The front door of the church is open daily and visitors are welcomed and invited inside to pray or to enjoy the silence. The embrace of calm peace is a very restoring experience and I accepted the invitation to step within. The Bible was open at Jeremiah and almost the first words I read were: 'Oh that I had in the wilderness a lodging place of wayfaring men.'

Aberlemno village is at the start of the Angus Pictish Trail which traces more than twenty Pictish sites throughout the county. On the trail, you can visit gloriously carved Pictish symbol stones and memorials with battle, hunting and biblical scenes. Close to Aber-lemno churchyard cross, there are three other roadside stones.

The church at Aberlemno was dedicated by Bish-op de Bernham in 1242 when most travellers went on foot. I like to think that, in the centuries since its dedication, it has been, if not a lodging place, then certainly a place of spiritual and mental renewal for wayfarers who accepted the invitation to stop awhile.

Not content with one churchyard, I also visited what I have always known as Beattie's Grave but the council signpost now calls it Kirkside Cemetery, just along from the nature reserve centre at St Cyrus (north of Montrose). I wanted to see if there were any graves of salmon fishers who had been employed on the salmon nets which used to be such a feature of St Cyrus Bay and provided employment for so many men.

Many of the gravestones are almost illegible because of lichen or the ravages of the weather but I found two. One deceased is referred to as a 'salmond' fisher. I looked this up in my *Jamieson's Etymological Dictionary of the Scottish Language* and, sure enough, it's there as an alternative to salmon. So Alex Salmond, the SNP politician, could just as readily be Alex Salmon – which just helps to fuel up my fascination for words.

Early August - Ecological

Something blue has been catching my eye every time I turn into the drive of the house. I thought it might have been a field of lupins but I'm learning not to make hasty assumptions so I phoned to check with Alan Stewart, the factor and farm manager.

'I know what you're calling about,' he said, greeting me with admirable intuition. I'd been looking at an acre of phacelia.

A most interesting crop, it is grown for several uses but this particular plot was planted to attract bees for honey production. When you get close to it, it has a stunning bloom like a blue flash which seems to almost vibrate in the air. There were plenty of bees foraging for nectar and lots of other insects attracted by the sweetness. I could hear the muted buzzing of all the little wings.

Talking to another farmer, Sandy Brown at Reidhall, I was wondering why oilseed rape is cut with a stubble about a foot high and barley is cut almost to ground level. Sandy patiently explained that the barley is cut and threshed by the combine harvester in one programme and then discharged into a bogey (trailer). Oilseed rape, topped off with its seedpods which contain the crop, is first cut with a swather into swathes, which must be left to dry. The straw lies on the tall stubble which lifts it away from damp earth and protects the crop. Several weeks later, when the seedpods have dried, they are put through the combine harvester and the tiny black seeds, much smaller than black peppercorns, are threshed out.

It's all so obvious when you have someone knowledgeable to help you through the hoops!

There's been an abundance of wild raspberries in the woods and I was able to pick nearly four pounds before the heavy rains spoilt the tail end of them. I got quite a picking of yellow rasps which I was delighted with as you usually only find an isolated bush or two at any one time.

As with wild strawberries, we have the raspberries as a delicious accompaniment to half an Ogen melon. There's nothing original about scooping the seeds out of half a melon and filling the cavity with other fruit – I'm sure loads of people do it – but the real treat is using wild fruit, which doubly enhances the experience. First there is the pleasure and satisfaction of picking your own fruit in the countryside – manifestly the fruits of your own labour – and then there's the contrast of the sweetness of the melon with the bitter-sweet taste which the wild raspberries and strawberries bring to the dish. 'Very spoilatious', as the Doyenne would say.

A call from Angus Davidson, who retired from farming at Glen Effock, an offshoot of Glen Esk, had the Doyenne and me hurrying up the glen to the annual Lochlee Games and Picnic at Tarfside. There was the usual friendly atmosphere about the occasion which always makes it such fun to be part of and Angus thought the turnout was the best in living memory. One mother got it right when she described it as 'just a lovely family day out and not a million miles from home'.

We took Macbeth along for the outing and he got tremendously excited at all the activity and races – so much so that he forgot himself and raised his leg against the Doyenne's shoe. I didn't know where to put myself.

Macbeth's liberality with his favours reached its peak when a tradesman called at the house. Our bold boy trotted out to welcome him and, perhaps because our visitor's dungarees smelt especially rural (we'll never know), raised his short, hairy leg against the visitor's trouser leg, and gave it a generous spraying. Not content with that, he turned round and, cocking his other hind leg with a flourish, concluded his welcome with a look of heartfelt satisfaction.

Late August - Border Tales

Two days of warm sunshine greeted us when we – the Doyenne and Macbeth, with me thrown in for good measure – visited La D's sister and her husband in their new home in Westmoreland. I noticed the emphasis is very much on the middle syllable, 'more'.

The M74, which becomes the M6 motorway, takes you down the west side of the country and reminds me in some respects of the A9 from Perth to Inverness. It's a real pleasure to drive through such noble hill country with glorious long views.

Once you reach the Border lands, it's a bit of a haunted country, full of old tragedies – from Flodden Field and the 'rough wooing' by Henry VIIII to the endless reiving from both sides of the Border. It's a wonder anyone ever lived there, it was such a wild place. H. V. Morton, in his seminal travelogue *In Search of Scotland*, described it as 'this queer compromise between fairyland and battle-field'. And it's that too – just think of 'Thomas the Rhymer and the Queen of Elfland' and Sir Walter Scott's *Minstrelsy of the Scottish Border*.

But we had no time to spare on such Homeric reflections as we had to get down to Long Marton in time for tea. It's a most attractive little village just off the A66. If we had carried on along that road, we would have come to Bowes, which I understand is where the Bowes family line of the Bowes-Lyons of Glamis Castle originated.

We were in Pennine country and specifically the Howgill Fells which have names such as Knott, Crook and Winder Fell. I had expected that the harvest would have been a lot further forward than up in Angus but there seemed to be a lot of combining still to be done.

On Saturday, we were taken to Orton which has a busy monthly Farmers' Market just like Forfar. We were close to original Cumberland sausage country so they would want to make a proper show but I was much impressed by the sausages on sale, which seemed to be several feet longer than we were used to.

A plain stone building was billed as Orton Liberal Club 1888. I was tickled by the carving of William Gladstone's head which appeared above the door lintel. It was a fine reminder of Fasque House, near Fettercairn, which was his Scottish home. There can't have been many Liberals in Orton because it's an awful wee hall.

There were plenty of new walks for Macbeth to explore and he enjoyed going out with Jess the Border collie for company.

After church, we were introduced to the retired Suffragan Bishop of Penrith who lives in the neighbouring village of Milburn. He told me Milburn had been built as a fortified village for protection against the marauding Scots, which seemed just how it should have been.

Bring forrit the tartan!

Autumn

September - Sunshine

Macbeth saw it first and took off across the lawn. From his body language, I guessed it might be a pheasant so I called him back to heel and he returned somewhat reluctantly.

The Doyenne and I were in the garden enjoying a glass of wine and the fading warmth of a glorious day's sunshine. We were watching the birds feeding on the peanuts and seeds. Most have become so accustomed to human and dog company that they take next to no notice of us.

One of our woodpeckers rocketed into the rowan tree beside the bird table. They are shy birds and we hoped, if we sat quite still, it would start feeding. However, Macbeth doesn't know the meaning of sitting still and the woodpecker was too wary to hang around.

But back to the pheasant – as, indeed, it was. About a dozen paces away a cautious head, with wattle-red patches around the eyes, was poking just above the cover of the long grass, spying out the prospects for supper. It was the cock pheasant that calls each day to feed on the scattered seeds below the bird table. With the three of us so close, he obviously had misgivings about leaving the safety of cover and coming into the open to feed. Finally, losing heart, he flew off across the potato field with loud 'klocks' of disapproval.

The Doyenne has made this year's rowan and apple jelly with rowans and apples from the garden. We had to supplement the rowans with some from the glen because the birds, especially the blackbirds, are devastation on them.

The elderberries (whose flowers provide the ingredients for the elderberry cordial) are almost over and have been a great attraction, especially for the pigeons. I hoped the Doyenne would try her hand at making elderberry jelly but she was reluctant, thinking it might taste very bitter. Perhaps next year, in the spirit of original research, I should have a go myself. I'll need to find a recipe first.

The rowan jelly has set well and the next treat to look forward to is seeing a generous spoonful on the side of the plate, embellishing several thick slices of good Scotch lamb.

From time to time, I've introduced our grandchildren into these Saturday pieces. I'm very happy to introduce the latest – granddaughter Mathilda is just four weeks old and, in the course of events, will, doubtless, have an increasing impact on our lives.

Our neighbour Ronald has built a 'sitooterie' – an invention of my Loanhead auntie, a sitooterie is a place 'oot in which you sit' to enjoy the fine weather – in a sheltered corner of his garden so that he and his wife can enjoy the summer sunshine and be protected from any chill winds. I called by to give it a trial and I must say he has chosen his spot well. However, I should have arrived an hour earlier when the iced coffee was on the go!

From the Doyenne's Kitchen

ROWAN AND APPLE JELLY

This is delicious served with game dishes and roasts, especially roast pheasant and lamb, and is known as 'meat jam' by the grandchildren. Rowans alone would be rather bitter so the addition of apples softens and enhances the flavour.

2 lbs rowan berries
2 lbs apples (some recipes use eating apples but I always use cookers)
4 pints water
2 lbs sugar

Method

Put the rowan berries, quartered whole apples (unpeeled and uncored) and water into a large saucepan. Simmer and cook with the pan half covered for 35–40 minutes or until the berries are soft and can be squashed against the side of the pan. Strain the liquid through a jelly bag into a bowl and leave it overnight. Put the liquid into a clean saucepan, add the sugar and heat gently until the sugar dissolves. Now bring it to a fast boil and continue cooking until you get a set. Put into warmed jars and seal.

October - Healthy Eating

Original ideas don't come along too often but the initiative started by Andrew Greaves, minister of Dundee West Church opposite the Art College, has tapped into a real need within the community and has been gathering rapid support.

Every Friday, between 11.30 a.m. and 1.30 p.m., in The Bridge Hall adjoining the church, the Healthy Cooking Co-operative volunteers invite everyone passing the hall to join them in 'Sharing the Harvest'. For only 50p, you can buy a nourishing lunch of a piping-hot bowl of soup with a slice of bread and, depending on what's available on the day, a bit of pudding too.

I can vouch for the tastiness of the meal. I had 'Braw Broccoli Soup' which was 'thick enough to trot a mouse on', as my mother used to say! Followed by 'Oaty Betty' which is a delicious recipe for cooking apples with porridge oats, brown sugar and cinnamon.

Andree is the enthusiastic cook who leads the kitchen team and her mission is to encourage people to cook fresh

David Whitson and Edward Young, son of Lord Young
who was a Lord of the Court of Session.

And here's a hand, my trusty friend,
And gie's a hand o' thine . . .

Did it or did it not go to the Antarctic?

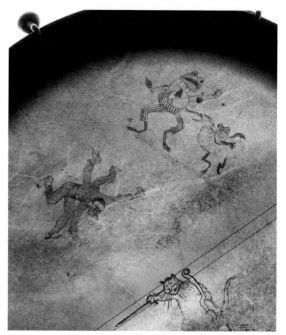

Dancing frogs and
'blacked-up' tap dancer
playing the 'bones'

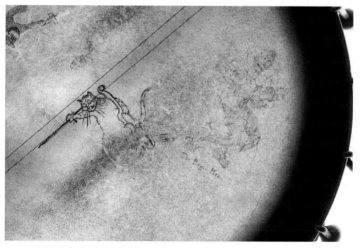

The cat and the fiddle and the bogeyman

Paying the rent at the fishing dinner
Pictured, left to right are: James Young, vet in Brechin; Gordon Officer,
farmer; Jim Scott, farmer and owner of fishing rights; Tom Whitson, solicitor
in Montrose; and Lewis (Lew) Thomson, owner of the Marykirk Hotel.
Unseemly mirth prevails!

produce that's grown and picked in its proper season. She gives a weekly demonstration to show just how easy all the recipes are, even for novices like me. To encourage healthier eating habits lunchers are given a free recipe sheet of what's been cooked on the day. I can't think where you'll get better value for 50p.

But it doesn't end there. A variety of fresh organic and non-organic vegetables – just whatever arrives on the day – is on sale at farm-gate prices. I bought four organic yellow courgettes (yellow ones were new to the Doyenne) and a monster head of broccoli for 63p. All the produce is locally grown and arrives practically with the dew still on it.

I spoke to Marie and Ellen, two art students from across the road who had heard about the project through word of mouth, and they were very enthusiastic about the availability of organic vegetables at student prices – and so close to the college.

It's an 'open-door' policy at The Bridge and everyone is welcome to pop in and learn more about a healthier lifestyle. There's a lot of support from senior citizens – they know a good deal when they see one – and it's obviously becoming a very social gathering. Judging by the noise level of the chat, the whole thing has been a runaway success.

The idea of 'Sharing the Harvest' was conceived as a partnership of farmers and the Scottish Countryside Alliance, with city folk. It highlights the interdependence and connection between country life and city life. Cooperation in this way between town and country helps city and rural communities to understand each other's points of view better.

The 'Sharing the Harvest' project has really found its place in the community. It has gone from strength to strength, attracting people of all ages, backgrounds and interests each week. After writing about it in *The Courier*, I took the idea to the BBC. Journalist and broadcaster Nancy Nicolson recorded a programme from the Bridge Hall for BBC Scotland's *Grassroots* – a radio programme which focuses on Scottish countryside issues, including food, farming and rural affairs. Afterwards, I was asked to assist with further research for the programme.

If you would like to find out what's good for you, a visit to The Bridge next Friday lunchtime should give you some nutritious ideas.

November - Glen Roadman

At least six families who have lived and worked in Glen Esk, at the northerly end of the county of Angus, for two or more generations are still there. They represent a strand of continuity that's unlikely to be found in many other glens. The primary school at Tarfside and the Masonic Hall, which doubles as the village hall, are just two of the glen's focal points to offer the kind of continuity that, I guess, makes people want to stay there.

Three estates, Invermark, Millden and Gannochy, the glen's farms and Scottish Water's waterworks at White-hillocks all provide people with regular employment. There's also seasonal work at The Retreat, the glen's folk museum, craft shop and restaurant.

However, one job disappeared some twenty-odd years ago – that of glen roadman. There actually used to be three roadmen – or 'lengthsmen', as they were also known – and each was responsible for a section (or length) of the glen's roads. So, when they announced the reintroduction of the glen roadman, there was a sense of welcome regeneration. Resurrecting the job has helped to ensure that Glen Esk remains one of the busiest and most populated Scottish glens. It has also restored locally delivered services to the glen.

I had a most interesting conversation with David Elliott who was appointed to the job of glen roadman in 2002. Although not originally from Glen Esk, he has lived there for ten years and has got to know it well. David's responsibility extends from the ancient church-yard at Loch Lee, at the very top of the glen, almost to The Burn House at the foot. His duties include clean-ing gullies and ditches to let water drain off the road, clearing up litter (which, in a better world, wouldn't be dropped in the first place) and cutting the grass in the churchyards and at the school and war memorial. The glen certainly benefits from his regular attention.

As I expected, being out in the open all day and be-coming part of the countryside means David is on the spot to observe the wildlife going about their daily business. Watching an otter dragging a salmon out of the river; seeing ospreys catch fish in Loch Lee; spotting an eagle attacking a deer calf; witnessing black cock and their strange courtship or 'lekking' displays; hearing bellowing stags during their mating or rutting season – these are things he is now familiar with.

David looks forward to the spring when the curlews and oystercatchers and peewits (a northern name for the lapwing or plover) start to nest. He sees green woodpeckers, which must be near to their northernmost limit in Scotland. And he once came across a barn owl in a deserted cottage, roosting on the handle of an old 'push' lawnmower.

It's easy to see why he loves his job. Most of us have to make special expeditions to get wildlife sightings like these – and, even then, it's only if we're lucky – but they are all there on David's doorstep and, from the way he speaks about his job, it's clear how much he appreciates the workplace which goes with it.

2004 – 2005

Winter

December - Miniature Train

Macbeth disappeared at speed, in pursuit of I know not what – but it was hot and it was beckoning! He was off up the track of the old Brechin to Edzell railway line and was deaf to my whistles and threats.

The county of Angus is criss-crossed with reminders of the small, branch railway lines that connected villages with larger towns and the main lines. With the advent of the railways, travel within the county became easier and quicker and produce and goods could be moved in bulk.

Many lines only survived for a few years and those that survived longer lost the battle in the 1960s, when Dr Beeching closed everything that couldn't show long-term viability. His legacy is the fretwork of disused tracks which are mini wildlife sanctuaries.

Although some sections were incorporated into agriculture, many old cuttings and embankments have been left to grow quite wild. Pesticide and chemical free, they provide cover for ground nesting birds and have become insect banks. Down at ground level, you can trace the runs and tunnels of small mammals and they are shelter for rabbits and hares and roe deer.

It was quite common for landowners selling their ground to the railway companies to include, as a condition of the sale, the provision of a private station for their families' personal use. One example of this was the Letham Grange station near Arbroath, the remains of which can be seen from the bridge over the main Aberdeen–London line, on the road from St Vigeans to Letham Grange House.

Ros Fletcher, whose family owned the estate, has told me that her great-grandmother was the last of the family to make use of the arrangement. Whenever she wished to travel, a message was sent to the railway company, probably the LNER at that time, and the train stopped to allow great-grandmother and her maid to board it. The branch line from Arbroath to Forfar passed through the estate. Ros and her sister, Mrs Sue Cooke, remember it when it had already been closed to traffic but they used to play amongst carriages which were stored on the disused line.

In the late nineteenth century, a private, narrow gauge railway was built at Letham Grange, possibly as a way of showing off the estate. Nothing remains of it now although the coal tender was used by the Fletcher family as a log basket. They would love to know where it has got to.

Ed Dutch, who owned the post office and shop at Craigo, told me his uncle was head gardener at Letham Grange and Ed remembered, as a very small boy, being given a ride on the miniature train.

It's a brisk, sunny autumn-like morning and, although last night's frost is still on the grass, it's just the morning to take Macbeth on another wild walk along the old railway line.

January - Native Scottish Wildcat

Macbeth pounced on what looked like a dead rabbit lying by the roadside. But it uttered two pathetic yowls and turned out to be a kitten, frost covered and frozen, and seemingly at death's door. I picked it up and it flopped over my arm, as though a car had struck it and it hardly had a whole bone left in its body. But I could feel warmth from it glowing through several layers of clothing and I thought the poor beastie was entitled to another chance.

I jumped in the car and took my patient to Laurencekirk Veterinary Hospital where vet Mike Robson examined it carefully and could find no broken bones. It was pretty far gone but Mike thought it worth giving it an injection and putting it in the incubator. The following morning, like a concerned St Bernard, I called again to see 'Angel', as she had been christened. She was still wobbly on her legs but was taking milk through a dropper. Everyone at the hospital seemed delighted with her progress and one of the veterinary nurses had decided to adopt her as a family pet.

She was a feral cat from a very late litter and Mike reckoned she was either parted from or abandoned by the mother who probably had problems feeding the whole litter. That would certainly explain why she was such a bag of skin and bone when I picked her up. The latest news of Angel is that, after a somewhat confusing introduction to domesticity, she's flourishing. I'm sure regular food and a warm bed are more than enough to soothe even a savage wee breast such as hers! She's a very lucky kitten – not least because she chose to collapse on a quiet lane with very little traffic. My thanks go to Mike Robson for his timely first aid.

In due course, I got a letter from the nurse who had taken Angel home as a pet:

> I am writing on behalf of Angel – or Holly, as she is now known. After a few weeks at home, my fiancé and I decided that Angel just didn't quite suit her very loud personality.
>
> The first few months with Holly were difficult as she was very much the feral cat we had thought. But a lot of perseverance and elastoplasts have paid off!
>
> As you will see from the photos enclosed she has made herself quite at home. She has learnt how to play – her favourite game at the moment is to wind up my two dogs.
>
> She has become a very loved part of our family so I would like to thank you for being kind enough to help her.
>
> Yours thankfully

The Doyenne and I are not cat people so I'm pleased to know my foundling has a secure future in a caring home.

All this excitement with cats in the wild got me thinking about true Scottish wildcats, which some people say no longer exist as a pure strain because of years of interbreeding with domestic and feral animals. I spoke to the head keeper of an estate that stretches well into the lonely places and hinterland of the east Grampians. He told me that, on their low ground, the 'wild' cats they see now are seriously hybridised because of interbreeding. In the more remote parts of the estate, however, they come across cats that have much more of the distinctive markings of true wildcats. Just like any animal, they want a bit of security and are found haunting rocky outcrops and cairns where there are caves and shelter. However, he reckoned that scientific research was now probably the only way to establish for sure whether the true native Scottish wildcat still exists.

February – Seashore and Semi-Precious Stones

An Irish girl told me that last Tuesday was St Brigid's Day and that the Irish traditionally regard the first of February as the first day of spring. The fair saint would have got a healthy suntan if she'd spent the day in our garden and, with Irish luck, it was a foretaste of what was to come.

Last Saturday was another sunny and settled day

so Macbeth and I took ourselves off to Usan, just south of Ferryden, which has always been a favourite haunt.

Driving down to Mains of Usan farm, I saw three herons at the side of the dam just above Inverusan House. I have a vested interest in that house. I spent the first six months of my life there until the family moved to Montrose because wartime petrol shortages meant my father spent too much time walking to and from Montrose and his solicitor business. It was known as Usan Cottage then and I still can't get used to calling it by its new name. I believe it was built as the dower house for nearby Usan House.

From the names Mains of Usan, Fishtown of Usan, Seaton of Usan, you'll realise that the Usan estate has the sea as its east march. I once saw a hare, that was being chased by dogs, jump off the rocks at Mains of Usan and swim for safety to a rocky islet. There's a blowhole on the same rocky shore which explodes quite spectacularly in a fountain of seawater when large incoming waves are forced through it. As a youngster, I spent many happy hours, armed with a fishing net, scrambling about the rock pools catching sticklebacks and crabs.

We walked along the shoreline towards Scurdie Ness Lighthouse. Facing the sea is a wee brae face of whins and rough grass which I've always known as The Rascal. You'd wonder why such an unimposing scratch of land, which can't even be cultivated, should have had a name and an identity long before I was born and which folk will remember it by long after I am gone – and forgotten too!

The warmth of the sun was too tempting and I lay down at the top of a bank overlooking the shore and closed my eyes. The sound of the waves breaking on the shingle had the same calming effect as the wind in the high branches of the trees round our house.

As we walked back along the shingle I spoke to a man bent double, searching for agates for which this stretch of coast is famous. He was obviously an enthusiast for he told me he'd come down from Maud, near Peterhead, and sometimes he went as far afield as the Ochil Hills, down Stirling and Alloa way.

Spring

March - The Wild Geese Depart

Winter withers and spring gathers pace. The days are lengthening and it gets easier to contemplate bounding out of bed and making the best use of the whole of the day although my good intentions were sorely tested with the dreich mornings we had at the start of the week.

Spring has really arrived for me when I see the delicate blue scilla flowers, which are about the last spring bulbs to bloom. Solitary little flowers which grow in ones and twos, they are a wee glint of colour when the snowdrops die away. Daffodils are still flowering in the woods. They come on later than the garden ones probably because the garden is more sheltered and sunnier. When I buried the Sheba dog last year, I transplanted a bunch of daffodil bulbs into the grave. They are looking well now and are a fitting memory to an old friend.

You become aware of changes in the routines of birds and animals at this time of year. Love may be in the air but so is wildlife's instinctive urge to breed and perpetuate each member of nature's family.

It is months since I noticed a hare in the fields round the house but yesterday morning I saw five in the winter barley. I came on them too suddenly to be able to take cover and watch them and they spied me straight away. One flapped down, characteristically flattening itself against the earth with its long ears laid along its back. If the barley had been just a little higher it would have disappeared from view. The other four sat on their haunches with their big radar ears flickering. Each side eyed up the other. I suppose Macbeth is enough to unnerve the boldest hare because soon they all cantered off, running mad March rings around each other and not really caring about us once they were on the move.

As the Doyenne was filling the log basket she found a field mouse which had crept into the log stack and died. We presume it was seeking shelter during the last snows but couldn't get deep enough to escape the deadly chill of the wind.

I was enraged several weeks back to find another hit-and-run dead red squirrel on the roadside. What made it worse was that its mate was sitting at the foot of the beech hedge . . . waiting.

I sometimes see the survivor foraging amongst the fallen beech mast and stop the car to watch it, scarcely a yard away from me. If they are regularly fed, squirrels readily become acclimatised to humans so this one was being very trusting – which was what did for its mate. Neighbour Ian has given me a video of the squirrels in his garden running around his feet.

We are well blessed with the number of red squirrels in our woods. I wish drivers would take just 10 mph off their speed when driving along the narrow country roads where these pretty animals are most frequently seen. It would give the squirrels more time to escape and drivers would have more time to avoid them.

As winter departs so do the geese. I hardly hear them now. I miss their wild calls for a week or two but I'm soon diverted by spring's messages of renewal.

PS Usually it's me who fills the log basket and carries it indoors!

Early May – Border Country and Recycling a Bridge

The Doyenne and I had a hectic long weekend down at Hexham, on grandparenting duty. Oldest grandson James came with us to visit his cousins Cecily and Fergus. Sharing all the interesting sights and stories with him, especially around the Borders, added to the fun of the journey.

We pointed out the triple peaks of the Eildon Hills where King Arthur is said to sleep, awaiting the call to ride out with his Knights of the Round Table and rescue all the maidens in distress, imprisoned in the topmost chambers of all the peel towers.

The Eildon Hills and the district round about are very much the heart of Sir Walter Scott country. Abbotsford, the house he built on the banks of the River Tweed lies halfway between Melrose and Selkirk. The famous Scott's View from Bemersyde Hill, westwards over the Eildon Hills, is worth the effort of a visit. You'll understand why Sir Walter stopped his horse, whenever he passed this spot, to sup up the stunning landscape.

There is a touching story of Sir Walter's final journey to his burial in Dryburgh Abbey. His favourite horse was drawing the carriage carrying his coffin and, from force of habit, stopped unbidden at the viewpoint his master loved so much. It took more than death to break the bonds of unspoken companionship between master and horse.

When we stopped on the Border itself, James liked the idea of standing with one foot in England and the other still in Scotland. As we neared Hexham, he told us about Hadrian's Wall which he had learnt about at school. We'll explore a bit of it the next time we go down.

Son Robert and his family live close to Hexham Racecourse and their house is surrounded by racehorse paddocks. All around, we heard the bubbling calls of curlews, which are at their noisiest during the breeding season. The birds have obviously been plentiful locally for a long time because a neighbouring cottage is called Curlew Cottage. Just outside the village of Rothbury, we saw a sign to Wagtail Farm so these attractive little bobbing birds must also have been a feature of the district for many a year.

On one of our walks, I taught James how to make a whistle by stretching a blade of grass between my two thumbs and blowing on the grass to make it vibrate. At the first piercing screech, a hare got up almost beneath the Doyenne's feet and took off across the field. We all had a look at the 'flap' it had made for itself in the grass, where it had lain, pressed flat along the ground, hoping we'd never notice it and pass on by.

The big expedition was to Cragside House, near Rothbury, an extraordinary Victorian pile built on the side of a crag. It has a quite overpowering marble fireplace, about the size of a village hall. It weighs ten tons and had to be built on to the rock so that it would be adequately supported.

Cragside House is now a National Trust property. It was built by the famous Victorian inventor, Lord Armstrong, of Vickers-Armstrong fame. It was the first house in the world to be lit by hydro-electricity that was produced by generators on the estate. Its other claim to fame is that it is reputed to have the tallest Douglas fir in England. These towering trees were introduced to Britain by David Douglas who is buried in Scone Old Parish Kirkyard, just outside Perth. David Douglas was one of the celebrated Victorian Scottish plant hunters who travelled the world and contributed so much to our woodlands and gardens.

On a totally different tack, I went to a presentation on the progress of the replacement bridge being built over the River South Esk at Montrose. I thought there might be something to hear about the effect of the building works on the wildlife but disturbance seems to be minimal. The duck, in particular, and the migrating salmon passing up the river appear to be quite unaffected by man's intrusions. What impressed me most was hearing that the engineers can use the original approach causeways on either bank, built in 1829 for the original stone bridge, to carry the new road over the river. Now, there's recycling on a grand scale!

Mid May - The Pirate and the Pig

After a lifetime's experience of dogs, I'm no longer surprised by the revolting things that they discover in hedge bottoms and proudly retrieve to share with me or eat . . . or sometimes both. So, when Macbeth appeared chewing steadily, I knew it was just some more of the same. This time, however, he had no intention of surrendering his treasure and nor was he willing to come to heel. There was a bit of undignified shouting and Macbeth played a bit of 'catch me if you can' – so I did. He sat there with his jaws clamped tight shut but I've been through all this kind of nonsense before and I soon prised open his mouth.

Out popped what looked like a bit of old tyre. It was the little orange rubber band round one end that gave me the answer. He had been gnawing on a lamb's tail. The bands are applied about half way up lambs' tails soon after birth to constrict the flow of blood beyond them. Eventually, the end of the tail shrivels up and drops off. Docking them in this way is quite painless and helps keep their rear ends clean once they are adult.

I got word that, after a season's break, there was an oystercatcher nesting again in the gravel on the round-about on the outskirts of Brechin. I went to have a look and there she sat, quite composed, with traffic whizzing past scarcely four feet away from her.

All the recent reminiscing about VE Day celebrations sixty years ago brought back a memory of our honeymoon forty years ago. The Doyenne (although in those halcyon days we'd no idea she was one) and I stayed at Renvyle House Hotel on the Connemara coast where the next stop is America. Well, not quite – Inishbofin Island lies about one and a half hour's sail off the coast and was where Oliver Cromwell imprisoned the Irish clergy after he had duffed up Ireland. It's not a big island but it has a real pirate's castle. There's also a pub which, forty years ago, had a very friendly pig which wandered in and out greeting the tourists. The pig was a bit of a psychologist and it waited till we were comfortably settled with our backs against an upturned boat and about to eat our packed lunch and then reappeared with a smile on its face which plainly said it would be pleased to join us.

A family from Aberdeen, also holidaying at the hotel, made the boat trip too. The whole point of this rambling story is that, on the sail to Inishbofin, one of the young sons looked me over and asked, 'What did you do in the war, Mr Whitson?'

I suppose it was my newly acquired marital responsibilities that made me seem so seasoned!

Late May - Ancestors and Orkney

Raking over old bones in search of ancestors was one of the reasons the Doyenne and I have just spent a week's holiday in Orkney. My paternal grandmother was born in Kirkwall and brought up, we think, on a farm several miles outside the town. Because of duplication of place names we need to do more research.

Some years ago we spent a long weekend in the Northern Islands, as they are known, and promised ourselves we would go back. As so often happens, it has taken a lot longer to do so than we originally intended.

Orcadians come from Orkney, not Scotland. The islands' historic allegiances, going back to the Vikings, mean that they identify more with Scandinavia than with what is generally referred to as mainland Scotland. Tell an Orcadian you come from 'the mainland' and they'll assume you are from Mainland Island, Orkney, which is how that island appears on Ordnance Survey maps. Cross the Pentland Firth and you land in what Orcadians call 'Scotland'.

The islands are a sublime experience. One day, we island-hopped and took the ferry to Sanday. We saw our first short-eared owl, which was hunting the dunes beside the nine-hole Sanday Golf Course. I'm not a golfer but it must be one of the most 'natural' links courses in the world. In addition to the usual hazards, it has a number of interesting animal by-products for players to avoid!

I was astonished to see ginger rabbits feeding in a field by the roadside. I spoke to a couple of farmers who told me they are a true mutant strain and not the result of interbreeding between wild animals and escaped pets.

Walking round North Loch, what I mistook for a skylark flew out of a clump of dried grass. In fact we had narrowly missed standing on a meadow pipit's nest containing five little brown marbled eggs.

Back on Mainland, we saw a great black-backed gull and what looked like one of its young sitting in a grass field. The immature gull turned out to be a great skua, which was another first for both of us. Both birds are great scavengers and, lying between them, was the carcase of a lamb they had been feeding on.

Starlings are very common and I watched a pair landing and then disappearing. Remains of World War Two defence installations are everywhere and this pair of birds had nested underground, beneath the cracked concrete base of a demolished hut. Normally, they nest on cliffs or high buildings but, in the absence of a more suitable site, they had adapted to local conditions.

Because Orkney has so few hills you are very aware of the infinite light which mantles the islands. That and the profuse yellow splashes of primroses on brae faces and along roadsides and ditches are the two enduring memories . . . until the next visit.

Summer

Early June – Legacy of the RNLI

Last Saturday, a new D-class lifeboat was handed over to Montrose Royal National Lifeboat Institution Station. It's an inshore boat for working in shallow waters where *Moonbeam*, the forty-seven-foot Tyne-class boat, cannot operate.

The new boat is named *David Leslie Wilson* in memory of a keen sailor who never forgot the service which rescued him when his yacht foundered in the Solway Firth. Montrose RNLI Station has benefited from his legacy which reflects the universal pride and gratitude felt for this totally voluntary-funded service. For more than 200 years, the RNLI has touched the lives of countless sailors and their families.

About twenty years ago, I was rattling a collecting tin on Lifeboat flag day and a young woman pushed a £5 note into it. At the time, it was quite a sum to donate so I asked her if she was sure she meant to give so much. She told me that, if the Lifeboat Service hadn't saved her uncle during the Second World War, she might never have known him. How better to express affection for a much-loved relative than by helping the service which, unquestioningly, went to his aid in wartime's dangerous and uncertain conditions?

During the naming ceremony for the new boat, I recalled that there used to be a wet dock at Montrose Harbour. This was an inner dock with lock gates that could be closed to maintain a constant level of water when cargoes were being loaded and unloaded.

In 1969, HMS *Wolverton*, built by the old Montrose Shipbuilding Company in 1956, made a courtesy visit to the town and berthed in the wet dock. Clearance getting in and out of the dock was scarcely a hand's span on both sides and, when she came to leave, she had to inch out, stern first, under almost no power.

The tide draining out of Montrose Basin and flowing past the harbour reaches a speed of up to eight knots – which is very fast. As *Wolverton* cleared the wet dock gates, she was caught by the full force of an outgoing ebb tide. Suddenly a very large ship was being whirled, like a leaf, across the river, towards the old pier at Ferryden (now known as Nicoll's Knuckle, honouring the late Alec Nicoll who for many years was the lifeboat Launching Authority). As the speed of rapidly changing events dawned on *Wolverton*'s crew, bells rang, lights flashed and matelots waved their hands in a frenzy of semaphoric lower-deck fluency. After a tremendous threshing of white water at the blunt end, she finally gained mastery of the tide and, thankfully, made her way safely down the river and into open sea.

If it had all gone belly up in the water and *Wolverton* had landed up on the Ferryden shore, all that the lifeboat crew would have needed to do to ensure the preservation of life was provide several long ladders!

The Doyenne's brother, who, at the time, was a captain in the Royal Artillery, joined HMS *Wolverton* at Montrose as part of a familiarisation programme before starting his staff college course at the Royal Naval College, Greenwich, as an exchange officer with the navy. As the ship left port and the scenario developed, the sole representative of Her Majesty's land-based forces could be seen standing, lonely, on the afterdeck, wondering where the lifebelts were – and pondering whether the naval tradition of the captain going down with the ship applied to gunner captains.

PS The navy do throw great parties.

Late June – Scottish Painters and Scottish Seals

The inevitability of the sea in its differing moods has been depicted by generations of storytellers and painters. Restless, caressing, serene, lonely – those are just a handful of defining adjectives used to portray it.

There's a spirituality in the sea which artists respond to. I think of Joan Eardley's wild seas beating on the rocks around her north-east home village of Catterline and of my great-grandfather Joseph Henderson's many, many seascapes and those too of his close friend and son-in-law, William McTaggart. But, for me, the sea's inevitability is perhaps best summed up by David Pullar, salmon fisher at Fishtown of Usan, when he speaks of being as 'patient as the sea'.

The sea has all the time in the world – the tide ebbs and the tide flows in its own ineluctable cycle. It would be wonderful to be as patient as the sea and to be assured today that what one expects tomorrow will indeed occur. The sea needs no such reassurance for nothing man can do will interrupt the cadence of its rhythm.

There are moments when I need to be near the sea. I bundle Macbeth into the car and, as often as not, we drive down to Kinnaber and then follow the riverside path down the River North Esk and so it was recently.

He and I sat, most companionably, on the sand dunes looking out over Montrose Bay and St Cyrus Bay, watching the ebbing tide drift gently away from the shore, leaving a damp strand of sand and pebbles.

There was still warmth from the setting sun on my back and I was content to lose myself in the measured beat of waves breaking on the shore.

I was in a dwam, away in a world of my own, and Macbeth broke into it. He sat bolt upright and was staring keenly out to sea. A seal's head, glossy in the evening sun, had popped up beside a salmon net arrowing out from the shore, set by the netsmen to harvest the king of fish. A second sleek head appeared beside another net. It was suppertime for seals and salmon is rich fare. Rather than devour the whole fish, a seal will bite choice bits out of it and move on to catch another one, leaving behind a trail of depredation and vexation.

The Doyenne was away on business for a couple of days, leaving me to 'bothy' on my own. She travelled by train and, as I put her on it and met her from it, I thought how there can scarcely be another railway station with a bonnier backdrop than Montrose. The Montrose Basin has such an abundance of birdlife and the light and the colour carry the eye away to the Grampian Hills. I've known it all my life and we're truly lucky to live in such a magical part of the country.

July – Inka and Whisky

All lugs and legs – that's Inka, the new member of the household. Born on 5 May, he's a black Labrador puppy who is already showing lots of spirit.

In much the same way we judge youngsters by comparing them to their parents, so Inka is very much a chip off the old block. When we went to see the litter, we got such a friendly greeting from the mother. Mind you, the pups were eight weeks old then and she may just have been delighted to see someone else taking an interest in them and giving her some respite. We also know two of the grandparents so it's good to have some practical knowledge of the pedigree.

It's been more than a year since Sheba died and I've missed the company of a bigger dog. Macbeth has been a great wee companion and there will be plenty more good times to come. Right now, he would like nothing better than to see this latest blot on the landscape sent straight back to where we got him from!

We're working hard to ensure that Macbeth doesn't feel rejected. Tickle one, tickle both. Talk to one, talk to both. I think what irks him most is that the puppy gets a midday feed and he doesn't. As the Doyenne says, it's like bringing a baby home and making sure the other bairns don't take bad with it.

Inka's Kennel Club name is Edradour Egret. Edradour is a delightful distillery outside Pitlochry. It's Scotland's smallest distillery and I had the opportunity to go round it about twenty years ago. My recollection is of compact, low, whitewashed buildings and everything being neat and tidy. It wasn't a long tour so each step of the distilling process was easily related to the previous one.

Egrets are birds with all-white plumage which is pretty much at odds with our all-black dog. It would be too confusing for a puppy to learn to respond to 'Edradour Egret'. I'm sure we've chosen a much easier name for Inka to get accustomed to. It's good to be a man with two dogs again and no longer writing under false pretences. We've lost nothing by taking so long to find Sheba's replacement and now we're looking forward to many years of fun with our twa dugs.

Walking in the woods I'm seeing the selective effects of the late, hard frosts we had in May. Some geans (wild cherries) and rowans will produce little or no fruit this year yet neighbouring trees seem unaffected. The beech hedges have suffered too. Brown autumn patches amongst the healthy green leaves show where the young growth was burnt by the cold.

And it's the same story in the garden. Last year there was a terrific crop of apples and plums. There will be pretty slim pickings here this autumn.

August – Genealogy

Making connections has proved to be a rewarding part of writing this weekly column. Shortly after I started in January 2003, Mrs Betty Bell wrote from Dundee to tell me that she had worked for my mother in 1942, when my parents moved from Forfar to Usan Cottage, near Ferryden. When I was six months old, the family moved to Montrose and Betty left to work elsewhere. So she had the dubious privilege of seeing me when I was not only wrinkled but pink!

It took a while longer for the next connection to emerge. I wrote in May that my paternal grandmother came from Kirkwall in Orkney. This jogged the memory of ninety-year-old Mrs May Christie of Arbroath who had worked for my granny when she lived in Forfar. My grandfather was a partner in the Forfar solicitor firm of W. and J. S. Gordon. It was Mrs Margaret Fletcher, also living in Arbroath, who wrote to me about Mrs Christie. By coincidence, Mrs Fletcher had worked for my father in the Montrose legal firm of Alexander Lyell and Son.

It's unlikely I would have met these ladies if I hadn't been writing my Saturday pieces. What's been so interesting is talking to people who can share their memories of my parents and my grandmother, which I would never otherwise have had.

A fortnight ago, I wrote about the great Marquis of Montrose. This prompted a letter from Mrs Jean Dundas whose late husband George was senior partner in the Kirriemuir legal firm of Wilkie & Dundas. Her interest is as a member of the 1st Marquis of Montrose Society whose aims are to raise awareness of the man himself and his impact on Scottish history. I remember George Dundas from my own short career as a solicitor, which ended in 1977. The added interest is that, before my grandfather David Whitson became a partner in W. & J. S. Gordon, he was previously a partner in Wilkie & Dundas.

Puppy walking with Inka takes up a lot of time. A passing cyclist stopped and commented on the new dog. He's a regular reader and knew about the addition to the household. As so often happens, we got talking.

He had grown up in the coastal village of Inverbervie, some twelve miles north of Montrose, and asked if I knew about 'Lucy Arnots' as this is the season for them. I'd never heard the expression but it's the Bervie name for pignuts or earthnuts. You'll see them on the roadsides and they have frothy, white flowers resembling ground elder. They have an edible tuber or bulb but be careful you know what you are eating if you are tempted to go digging for them.

I was confident I would get information about 'Lucy Arnots' from readers. An Arbroath reader sent a recipe for vegetable broth with pignuts from a book called *All Good Things Around Us* by Pamela Michael. The seventeenth-century *Compleat Herball of Physical Plants* suggests that the nuts are an aphrodisiac.

Old friend Arthur Grewar took me down to a riverside grass field to dig some. After cleaning and scraping the skin off them, I added them to a salad. They taste like a cross between raw chestnuts and fresh hazelnuts, with a hot aftertaste of radish. Scottish folklore has it that, if you eat too many, you will get head lice! Possibly this originates from the old name 'lousy arnuts' which appears in *Jamieson's Etymological Dictionary of the Scottish Language*.

Retired Mearns farmer Gordon Robertson tells a story about a Hebridean Highland chieftain who was gazing from his castle window. He saw his ploughman pluck a Lucy Arnot from the field and eat it. The chieftain picked up his musket and shot the ploughman stone dead. Although charged and tried with murder, he was found not guilty because the ploughman had stolen what was rightfully his chief's.

Hard times in them days!

Autumn

September - High Jinks in Marykirk

My Address to my Solicitor

Tae meet him, ye gang up a stair—
Deil tak' the ploy that leads me there.
The steps, as I ha'e coonted ower,
Cost two pence each or three and fower.
He writes me whiles a wee bit line
And says he is sincerely mine.
But, in a book, he's noted doon,
To writing you, say, half a croon.
I aften think it wad be braw
Gin I could do without the law.
But, when I'm in a fax, I ken
I'll climb thae twenty steps again.
Bit ae dull day wi' grave content,
He'll read my will and testament.
Ah, lad, I'll ha'e the laugh on ye—
Ye'll send yer bill bit no' tae me.

'My Address to my Solicitor' was penned for my father by
Lewis (Lew) Thomson who owned the Marykirk Hotel.

I often went there with Father who drank whisky but I was only old enough to be offered ginger beer. The poem contains a little bit of Scottish social history. 'Three and fower' is 3s and 4d (pre-decimal currency, for the very young!), which is half of 6s and 8d, which is one third of £1 or 20 shillings. And 6s and 8d was the standard fee for a consultation with your 'man of business' (a near-vanished description now) in the 1950s. Far off days but I did manage to track down a solicitor – and not as old as you might imagine – who remembered, as a law apprentice, writing up client ledgers and charging out such fees.

I believe Mr Thomson retired to Forfar after he sold the hotel. It would be interesting to know how much more of his lively poetry survives and, better still, if it was ever published. He obviously had a pawky wit and a way with words.

I have a photograph, taken in the Marykirk Hotel, of a fishing supper when the annual rent for sporting rights was handed over. Seated round the table are my father and Jim Young, who was the vet in Brechin, with Gordon Officer, who farmed Ardoch of Gallery. The men are seen paying their rent in bags of ha'penny coins to Jim Scott who farmed neighbouring Mains of Gallery and had the adjoining riparian fishing rights on the River North Esk. The figure with his back to the camera is Lew Thomson. Unseemly hilarity is very apparent.

I was woken about half past three in the morning by a noise I just couldn't place. So I got out of bed and prowled round the house. I eventually tracked it down to Inka – hiccupping. All the childhood remedies like drinking water from the wrong side of the glass or telling him to hold his breath and count to fifty would be wasted on him. Putting a cold key down the back of his neck would have been the opportunity for a great game which would likely have ended in the key being swallowed!

I could have waited until his attention was diverted and tried the ultimate cure of giving him a big fright. But it wisnae cosy out there and it was cosy in bed – so that's where I went back to.

October - Mixed Bag

I spent a fascinating morning with Councillor Bob Spink. A retired Arbroath fish merchant, he is an encyclopaedic authority on Arbroath – in particular, the fishing community. Bob has a wonderful collection of old photographic plates, recording the fishermen's lives in the fishing villages of north-east Scotland. They are the work of John Fraser, of the well-known Arbroath engineering family, and they cover the period from 1885–1915. As well as a historical record they are a social record too of work and dress, and of old buildings and their interiors.

It was the photos of Montrose that especially interested me. I recognised much of Montrose Harbour and the outline of the north bank of the River South Esk reminded me how that part of the town remained relatively unchanged until after the 1950s. And I recalled the fishermen's black, tar-painted net sheds that lined the riverside at Ferryden, the fishing village on the south bank of the river. One of the biggest changes is the new road bridge linking Montrose and Rossie Island, which has just opened to traffic. The bridge in Bob's photographs isn't just the one before this new one but the bridge before that.

Many of the fishermen have strong faces that are old before their time – lined with the hardships of their occupation. It's a temptation to look back from the comfort of life today and think there was a romance about life then. But those men went out in open sailing boats, in all weathers, and if the wind was against them, they rowed.

They say that fishermen are the last of the hunters. Bob says there's salt in his blood and that, even now, he could go to the fishing. I reckon that, if he ever feels the temptation getting too strong for him, he just needs to turn to his photographs to knock the wild fancy out of his head!

On the way home, I took the familiar wee road from Rossie Braes over Maryton Hill. I stopped on the brow of the hill because the view was just magic. Montrose Basin was full and the sun was sparkling on the water and on Montrose too. East of the town, I saw the grey line of the North Sea where the old fishermen, whose photographs I'd been looking at, had toiled to catch their silver harvest. To the west, the Angus hills looked fair and peaceful. And the strath that runs from Stone-haven to Perth was chequered with golden stubble fields, fresh green shoots of winter barley and brown where the tatties had been lifted.

There's been building and renovation going on next door and I wondered how it would affect the visitors to our bird table. I needn't have worried – the birds have just ignored all the extra activity. Even the woodpeck-ers, which are normally very timid, didn't stay away for long. And at night, when I go out last thing with the dogs, the tawny owls have returned to serenade us with their 'kee-wick, kee-wick' calls.

Early November – Morris Dancing and Quails

Morris dancers, with their straw hats and colourful rib-bons and bells, dancing their hearts out in the middle of Montrose High Street would always seem a bit out of context. But seeing them there at the end of October, waving their hankies and whacking away at each other with their sticks, stopped me in my tracks. What sur-prised me even more was that they had come down from Banchory, where there's been a Morris Dancing 'side' (technical term for a team) for the past thirty years.

I had a word with the young man who was collect-ing donations in his straw hat. He was wearing a rather natty horse costume, tastefully fashioned from fabric stitched over a frame. 'Horseman' told me that the earliest references to the dancing could be traced back to the time of James II of Scotland who died in 1460. As this seemed to be a hitherto unknown Scottish tradition, for me at least, I checked on the internet.

'Morris' is believed to derive from Moorish and Morris dancing was, indeed, first mentioned in the fifteenth century but I could find no references to Scotland – despite what 'horseman' said. Which was a relief because it would have been too much at odds with my perception of wild Highlanders, celebrating their battle victories by dancing reels and flings to the clamour of bagpipes.

In complete contrast, I've been learning a little about quail, which, up till now, I've known next to nothing about. They migrate here from Europe to breed and, apparently, the chicks which hatch in the springtime are ready to mate and breed by late summer. So it's possible for three generations of birds to fly back south in the autumn.

A big hit with youngsters at the annual Scottish Countryside Alliance's Countryside Festival at Glamis Castle was an incubator with quail eggs hatching. It allowed them to experience something totally natural, which they wouldn't normally see.

There are farms around Arbroath where they expect to see or hear an odd pair but, this past season, birds have been seen in almost every field. I'm told also that they are annual visitors on farms in the Fern area, between Brechin and Kirriemuir. And my father told me that two wee coveys used to appear each year among the bents on Kinnaber Moor, just north of Montrose.

Although I've never seen or heard them in the wild – they are about the size of a thrush – I have eaten them. They have a mild, subtle flavour that doesn't compare with other game birds. Hard-boiled quails' eggs, dipped in celery salt, are regarded as a special treat at parties. Real show-offs peel the shells between the thumb and forefinger of one hand.

The Doyenne buys eggs from Neil Watt, butcher in Montrose, who has a local supplier for them. So I should go and see them in captivity and I'll get to know a lot more about them.

Late November – J. M. Barrie Writes Peter Pan

'Klock, klock!' A cock pheasant was brazenly standing on the old wall outside the kitchen window, calling on the world at large to acknowledge that he was king of the castle. He's taken up post there for several days and is obviously staking a territorial claim to that part of the garden. It's 'a very good address' – as my mother would have said – for a pheasant. There's unlimited feeding at the bird table, it's a suntrap round the front of the house for its leisure moments and there are plenty of high trees nearby to roost in overnight. Macbeth gave up trying to fly some time ago so he's no threat, and Inka's just a hauflin.

And on the subject of dogs, Inka's discovered barking. He's still exploring his full range but appears to be the canine equivalent of a pleasing baritone. He can't make up his mind whether to show off his newly found skill or be embarrassed by its social consequences. We don't want yapping dogs every time someone comes to the door but it's reassuring to have a barking dog to warn folk inside, and callers outside, that someone's keeping an eye on things.

The Doyenne and I are enjoying a jar of Yorkshire honey which came as a gift from the Ryburn Valley and Moors. It's heather country round there so you'd expect it to be as lip-smackingly tasty as it is. We know where it came from and who produced it – 'traceability' they call it in the trade. It's so much more of a treat than some of the anonymous products bought off the shelf.

I was going through the last of my father's papers and came across two letters written by J. M. Barrie to my grandfather D. S. Whitson, who, for a time, was a solicitor in Kirriemuir, which was Barrie's birthplace. The house Barrie was brought up in now belongs to the National Trust for Scotland and it's an interesting place to take visitors. The washhouse on the back green was the inspiration for the Wendy House.

One letter is dated February 1904 and I like to think that the pen he used to write to my grandfather was the same pen he used to write *Peter Pan*, which had its stage premiere in December of the same year, at the Duke of York Theatre, London.

A much more exciting find amongst the papers, tucked away in an envelope, was a five-million-drachma banknote. I had to count the noughts several times to be quite sure what it was. Then I dashed to the bank, thinking all my boats had sailed in together. The bank returned it to me, pointing out that the date was 1944. It had been printed by the Nazis during their occupation of Greece during the Second World War. It was worth only what a collector would give me for it. Oh, the disappointment!

2005 – 2006

Winter

Early December - Wee Dappin

The Wideopen (its local adaptation used to be the 'Wee Dappin') is the old road that cuts off from the A937 just north of Marykirk and crosses over the hill to Kirkside, just south of St Cyrus. It's well named because it's rather bleak and wide open to the weather.

I started up the hill and four roe deer, which had come out of the woods, were grazing in the sun on the far side of the Burn of Balmakelly. One looked up briefly when I stopped to watch them but they knew they were secure from any disturbance. I watched a buzzard being mobbed by two crows until it could stand the aggravation no longer and flew off.

On the summit of the hill is Hospital Shields Farm. When I was very small, my parents knew the farmer whose name I'm sure was Pentland. I do remember he had a pocket watch. He would take it out of his waist-coat pocket to let me hear it ticking. The name and site suggests that there was a hospital where the farm is now. It could possibly have been where monks cared for fever victims well away from other habitations – a sort of local version of Soutra Aisle, the great medieval hospital built near the summit of Soutra Hill, on the road to Lauder.

It was a snappy, clear day and, to the east, the sun was bouncing off the sea opposite Montrose. Scurdie Ness Lighthouse and the spire on St Cyrus Church poked skywards. Fishermen and mariners must have welcomed such prominent marks to steer by in the days before GPS.

Then I went past the splendidly named Gaupies-haugh. I had to consult Jamieson's dictionary to find that 'gaupie' was a term for a foolish person – or 'wandered' as they might have said in days past.

I turned back on the A92, heading for the Lower Northwaterbridge and Montrose. Opposite the Stone of Morphie road end, there used to be the tiny station for Kinnaber Halt, on the single-line railway from Montrose to Johnshaven. There was a wooden gate on the roadside that you went through to get down to the single platform and, if you wanted the train to stop, you waved your hankie or tile hat to the driver.

I was a child when the railway line closed and, although I didn't go on the very last journey the train made, a lady called Lena, who helped my mother, did take me on its second last one. I wonder if she remembers that?

The actual Stone of Morphie stands in the steading of the farm of that name and is supposed to mark the grave of a Scots king killed in a battle with the Vikings. There are stories that a human skeleton does indeed rest beneath it.

It was just a morning revisiting all sorts of places I've known since childhood – 'remincing', as an old lady I knew used to say!

After writing about the Wideopen, I was most interested to get a note from a reader telling me that, as a young man, her father had walked that road every Sunday (about six or seven miles), with his dog for company, to court her mother who lived in St Cyrus. He got his lunch and, in the evening, he walked home again. The young couple must have taken other walks up the coast because the writer's first name is Finella which comes from Den Finella, an attractive wee glen that runs down to the sea just below Johnshaven.

I also learned that her cousin was Jimmy Maver. For some years, Jimmy and his wife Millie owned the post office and shop at Craigo, which was our local shoppie when we lived at Logie Pert. Jimmy's father was Bob Maver who was gamekeeper at Craigo Estate and I remember him too.

And the connections didn't end there. I got an e-mail from a man researching his family history. Through the weekly column, he had been able to trace his great-great-great-grandfather who had farmed Hospital Shields Farm till 1837.

Late December - Golf Balls

Golf balls should be on golf courses so I was surprised to find one when walking with dogs in a field not far from the Drovers Inn, near Memus. The nearest golf course is at Kirriemuir, about six miles away, so there had to be a logical reason for the pristine Slazenger golf ball doucely lying in the long grass. I'm sure it was humorist P. G. Wodehouse who wrote a story about a golfing challenge which involved driving a ball cross-country between two towns but that seemed an unlikely explanation in this case. There's the River South Esk to cross and several woods to negotiate where it would certainly have been lost.

Someone suggested there might be a golfing enthusiast tractor driver out there who swings a casual golf club when nobody is looking. A local laird opined that it was probably a crow that had picked it off the Kirriemuir golf course and flown off with it till it tired and dropped it where it lay.

Jackdaws are well known to carry off a wide range of objects but I should have thought a golf ball was a slightly tall order for one of the smaller members of the crow family. Carrion crows are also thieves and are quite capable of taking a golf ball. It's just that six miles seems an awful distance for even the most sporting crow to fly with such an improbable object.

Conservationist David Stephen wrote many fine wildlife articles and I pulled out his anthology, *Scottish Wild Life*, to see what he had to say. He didn't throw any light on my conundrum but told a delightful story about a farmer's young daughter who knew about carrion crows and thought they were so named because they were for ever 'carryin' things awa'!

As an afterthought to the golf-ball conundrum, I recall an item that appeared in *The Courier* about a ladies' golf competition on Kirkwall Golf Course, in Orkney. In the course of the game, crows stole six balls from the players so perhaps the local laird was right!

For a man with two dogs, I've neglected writing about them of late. The Doyenne took Macbeth to the vet for his booster injection and he – Macbeth, that is – is in good fettle. He's the right weight for his size and the only complaint, which can be corrected with a change of diet, is the rather lethal 'dog's breath' which he likes to share with you when he whispers in your face.

Inka is seven months old now and has all the bumptious confidence of a teenager. He's tormenting the life out of Macbeth. He thinks it's tremendous fun to race at his small friend and bowl him over and sometimes he's so rough I have to shout at him.

There's not such a bond between them yet as Macbeth had with old Sheba but she was twelve years old when Macbeth came to us and she became his surrogate mum.

Spring

Early March - Raptor Rapture and Green Sandpiper

A feathered bullet shot past the window. Even in that split second, I was certain it was a sparrowhawk and it was a first visit in over four years. Just quarter of a mile away, our neighbour Ronald often sees these aerodynamic killing machines patrolling the side of his wood. I've wondered why we don't see them here when the bird table offers such a choice of small songbirds for breakfast, lunch and tea. Possibly this was the first time I was in the right place at the right moment.

It was neighbour Ronald who pointed out the green sandpiper which appeared for about ten days at the side of the stream, about a hundred yards beyond the garden boundary. This was a pretty rare migrant visitor to Scotland and I feel quite lucky to have seen one. It's gone now – probably escaped from the snow to a warmer destination – but the frozen pond on the far side of the field sent six mallard duck to roost on the stream at the foot of the garden. No wonder I was hearing the whistle of their wings as they circled the house preparing to land.

I so enjoyed the snow lying for more than just a couple of days. It really seemed like proper winter weather. Last Saturday the sun shone out of a cloudless sky and the dogs and I took ourselves into Glen Esk. We walked through a stand of trees to higher ground, looking across to parts of the glen I don't normally see. The view was stunning and it lifted my spirits to be in such a peaceful place. Sunday was just as memorable and I sat outside for more than an hour, in hot sunshine, reading my book until my nippy toes reminded me it was frosty underfoot. The dogs, Macbeth and Inka, just love the snow and spent the morning sparring with each other and rolling about in it.

After lunch, the Doyenne and I drove over the Caterthuns and into Glen Lethnot, which adjoins Glen Esk. The two glens are quite different. Lethnot is bare and spartan compared to its neighbour but the snow changes the character of everything and highlights features you don't normally notice.

When they were young, we used to take the family up Lethnot for picnics and to paddle in some of the deeper pools of the West Water. And, if you're not as fleet as once you were, it's easy walking nearer the top of the glen.

Macbeth has had his spring clip. As usual he went in deep shagpile and came out cut moquette. Now that all the foliage has been cut back it's apparent that he is turning into Macbutterball. Some painful decisions may have to be taken about diet but he'll have the consolation of knowing the Doyenne and I are sharing the pain with him!

Late March - Eels and Old Nick

Eels have a special place in the dark recesses of the Scottish psyche. Why and when we developed a distaste for eating them is very much a mystery. It can't have always been so because there are still working eel traps and enough evidence of old ones in the county of Angus alone to make it clear that eels were an important item of diet at one time.

I spent an informative morning at Milldens Mill, between Friockheim and Forfar, being shown over the historic, and still working, meal mill and the eel trap which relies on the mill lade to provide its harvest of eels. Eel traps benefit from simplicity for their effectiveness. The Milldens one is nothing more than a large, square box lined with quarried stone slabs. It has an inlet from the mill lade and an outlet to carry away the water. The Lunan Water, which feeds the mill lade which, in turn, powers the mill, flows from Rescobie Loch through Balgavies (pronounced Balguys) Loch and down to Lunan Bay, between Montrose and Arbroath.

The eels are born in the Sargasso Sea, somewhere south of Bermuda. They come to Scotland as elvers, and feed and grow in our streams and ditches and lochs until they are mature. Then, like our salmon which return from Arctic waters to their mother rivers in Scotland to spawn, instinct tells the adult eels it's time to make the enormous journey from Scotland back to the Sargasso to start the whole mysterious reproductive cycle all over again.

Migration down traditional waterways like the Lunan occurs in September and October. Best catches are made on moonless nights, when river levels are rising and the water is turbid and clouded. These conditions may provide some sort of natural protection to help hide the migrant fish from otters which, after man, are their worst predator.

A series of grilles controls the eels' progress along the mill lade until the only way forward is through a pipe from the lade into the eel trap, from which there is no escape.

Up until the 1960s, and to a lesser extent the 1970s, eels were caught and smoked locally and I recall them fondly as a particularly delicious meal. But most went by train to Billingsgate Fish Market in London, or were transported in specially tanked lorries to the Continent. Declining catches mean that now it is more difficult to find regular markets.

So what is it about eels that makes our Celtic fantasies writhe? They are long and sinuous and serpent-like. Pick one up and it will wrap its tail and body round your hand and wrist like a tentacle. Worse still, they have slippery, slimy skins and can travel overland, usually during the uncertain hours of darkness. They surely can't be fish and snakes have reassuringly dry skins.

Maybe there's something about them of Old Nick himself that gives us the creeps.

April – Country Sports

Country sports are alive and well, I can report. Some are little known and others go into hibernation until someone resurrects them and everyone has a jolly good laugh.

The Doyenne and I had enjoyed a very convivial lunch party and I was quietly contemplating an afternoon snooze when we got home, when I found myself the victim for the after-lunch gamie. It wasn't one I had come across but it's been played by our host and his family for many years.

The trick is to get a postage stamp to stick to the dining room ceiling using a flat disc of plasticine as a means of propelling it there. If the stamp sticks, the plasticine falls away. The stamp was face down in the plasticine and I moistened the glue on the back before I threw it. It wasn't as easy as you might imagine – the missile had to connect full-face with the ceiling to ensure the stamp sticks, otherwise it and the plasticine would drop back down into my neighbour's coffee!

I'm pleased to report I succeeded first try and my stamp has the distinction of being the stamp nearest the ceiling rose. I didn't actually see its denomination but our host told me that the oldest stamp on the ceiling dates from 1937.

I've since heard of the stamp game being played with an old penny – or a 2p piece in today's currency – as the projectile.

Some years ago our host's family was in uproar when it was proposed to paint the dining-room ceiling. Such were the howls of protest that the painter was eventually instructed to paint round every single stamp, which probably tried his patience no end.

In the same vein, I made a 'stoorer' to occupy grandson James who spent some of his Easter holiday with us. I hadn't made one for over fifty years.

Take an old syrup or treacle tin, with a lid, and bash a few holes in the sides. Fix a piece of firm wire, about thirty inches long, through two holes opposite each other at the top of the tin, to form a handle. Scrumple up some small balls of newspaper and put them in the bottom of the tin. Fill the tin with pieces of rotten but tinder-dry wood – a walk in the country to find an old dead tree adds to the excitement of the whole event. Light the balls of newspaper, fix the lid on tightly and blow through the holes until the wood starts to smoulder and the 'stoorer' starts to smoke. Then wander round the garden, swinging the 'stoorer' round your head, until the wood burns out and the 'stoor' stops smoking.

And what's the object of this ploy? I haven't the faintest idea but the boy with the 'stoorer' gets to be the leader of the gang.

One warning, though – the tin gets very hot so it should always be kept away from and allowed to cool off well out of reach of small or unsuspecting hands.

May - Natural Remedies

Out and about with the dogs, I see plenty of evidence of spring's progress. I especially enjoy the wee flashes of blue and yellow in the woods and hedgerows. Common violets and speedwell and the early forget-me-nots have just enough time to announce their presence before they are shouldered aside by sprouting undergrowth. The field behind the kitchen is filled with petite yellow wild pansies or heartsease.

I did some research into the derivation of the country names for these wild plants, which have such grand Latin descriptions for such, mainly, tiny flowers. Heartsease was used to treat a wide range of afflictions. On the one hand, it was a laxative and, on the other, it was highly regarded as a love potion, which seems a bit of a contradiction. These wild pansies are also called love-lies-bleeding, which is another conundrum. However, they sound like powerful medicine and, if they were as efficacious as they sound, small wonder our ancestors experienced an easy heart as they looked forward to a rapid recovery.

A hapless knight was picking a bouquet of flowers for his lady love by the side of a rushing river. He slipped and tumbled into the foaming waters. As he was swept to his doom, he threw the spray of flowers back to his love with the fateful words, 'Forget me not!'

Speedwell was also traditionally valued for its medicinal properties. I learnt that it should be 'given in good broth of a hen' and that it was used as a specific against 'pestilential fevers'. It was an accepted cure for bronchial troubles but I like the idea that it was also widely used to treat 'the itch'. Mediaeval itch would have needed more than a good scratch if you wanted to get well speedily!

The *Speedwell* was, of course, the sister ship of the *Mayflower* (another traditional physic), which took the Pilgrim Fathers to America in 1620. John Whitson was Lord Mayor and Member of Parliament for Bristol and one of the city's merchant venturers or entrepreneurs. There is a family tradition that he was one-time owner of the *Mayflower* although, by 1620, he had sold her and the Pilgrim Fathers chartered her from the new owners.

The story is that *Mayflower* needed a new set of sails to complete the long voyage to the new world and the Pilgrim Fathers sought John Whitson's help. He agreed to supply the sails on condition the adventurers took Cheviot wool with them to trade for native goods, which would be sent back to England by way of profit.

It's unlikely old John was an ancestor for another family tradition is that the Scottish Whitsons are all descended from three Viking brothers. But it's a good story and there are enough grains of credibility about it to think it might be true.

Summer

June - Fishy Story

'Mother' nature is a bit of a misnomer sometimes. It's survival of the fittest out there with no tears shed over an early death or a life not even lived.

The dogs and I walk in two uncultivated stubble fields left in 'set aside'. It's great walking at this time of year because the stream runs between them and there's a wide variety of wildlife. I found an oyster-catcher's nest in amongst the stubble, open to the elements and predators. One egg hadn't hatched but at least one other did because we were regularly scolded by anxious parent birds the moment we went into the field.

We found a pheasant's egg which had been removed from the nest, possibly by one of the jackdaws which come to the garden during the nesting season. That was one chick that would never see the light of day. The egg was punctured and Macbeth was licking out the remainder of the yolk which dribbled out of the shell when I picked it up – just one example of the way that predators survive.

Further on, we came across two more pheasant eggs where chicks had obviously hatched. The empty shells had been dropped well away from the nests so as not to draw unwelcome attention to the fledglings. An empty partridge egg told a similar story of success.

A dead leveret lay unmourned on the road. They have a tendency to try to outrun cars as they seek an escape route so it's worthwhile slowing down to give them the chance to dart into the undergrowth.

Many years ago, commercial salmon fishers would, quite legally, pay a bounty for every pair of cormorant feet handed in to them. This was because cormorants – or 'scarts', as they're called locally – prey on young salmon as they make their way downriver to the sea. At two or three years old and about six inches (150 mm) long, the juvenile salmon or smolts begin their long journeys in April and May. The smolts congregate in large numbers at river mouths where they spend time acclimatising to the salt seawater before migrating to Greenland and the sub-Arctic northern oceans. After about three years of intense feeding, they return to their mother rivers to spawn.

Sometimes a fishy story comes along that's a bit hard to swallow. A man watched a cormorant fishing at the mouth of the River South Esk. When the bird rose from the water, he shot it. He opened it up to see what it had been feeding on and, inside, he found a freshly caught trout with a record tag attached to its fin. He handed the tag into the then Department of Agriculture and Fisheries, who paid him £1 for its return. He also received five shillings (25p) as bounty for the scart's feet from the local commercial salmon netting company and he ate the trout for his breakfast! I'm assured it all happened as it's told.

Reference made last week to not casting a clout till the month of May is out brought a response from a reader. Hawthorn blossom is called 'may' and country folk were cautioned not to discard their woolly long johns till the may blossom had fallen from the trees.

Early July – Silver Salmon – King of Fish

'Fish scales in the blood' well describes Bob Ritchie, son and grandson of salmon netsmen and himself still carrying on this traditional occupation.

The sun was shining, the temperature had risen and I had taken the dogs down to Kinnaber beach, north of Montrose, where they can really stretch their legs, free from any danger of traffic. I love the sea and should go down to it more often which, perhaps, is why these days are so special.

I found Bob changing a fishing net. 'Jumpers' they are called now and they are simplified versions of the old stake nets that I remember so well as a youngster. Fifty years ago the sandy beaches at St Cyrus, Montrose and Lunan Bay provided work for a small army of fishermen but the commercial salmon fishing industry is greatly reduced now.

Standing on the cliffs or the high sand dunes, you would see the arrowhead shapes of the nets poking out into the sea. These were and still are the catching chambers which trap the salmon. Fly nets they called the stake nets, locally. I have memories of the fishermen walking out along the net, like flies on a spider's web, which may account for the local term. With only a footrope and a handrope to steady themselves, they scooped the salmon out of the water with a long-handled, heavy landing net called a scum net.

The stumps of poles you can see along the tideline, blackened with the sea, are the remnants of these 'fixed engines', as they are called in the arcane language of the statutes enacted to regulate the industry. But they were manpower-intensive and couldn't survive the need for cost-cutting and fiscal efficiency. The jumpers, on the other hand, can be managed by just one or two people.

South of Montrose, at Usan, the Pullar family own the netting rights and three generations of this fishing dynasty work the nets. The coastline has changed to high cliffs and a rocky, boulder-strewn shore. Here they use bag nets which float permanently in the water. To empty them they must motor out in a salmon coble with its familiar and distinctive high prow.

Go down to the old limekiln at The Buddon and you'll see the orange buoys and long poles which support the nets in the water. If you're there about half tide, you may see the fishermen emptying them of the wild fish.

I know where several cobles are lying forgotten and deteriorating. I can't help thinking that one, at least, should be saved and restored as a memory to the boat-building skills and fishing traditions which supported so many men and their families on this part of the north-east. Perhaps there's an opportunity for Angus to lead the way in establishing a museum or heritage centre for the salmon fishing industry!

Late July – Thunder and Lightning

Both dogs slept blissfully through the cracks of thunder and flashes of lightning that awoke me at a thoroughly indecent hour.

When I was small, my mother sat me down at the window during thunderstorms to listen to the drum rolls and watch the flickering lights. As a result, I've always rather enjoyed storms and not hesitated to go outdoors during them. Like the wind and sea, lightning is a force of nature although few of us experience its full destructive power.

My father's friend from his schooldays, Willie Wyllie, whose family farmed Drumclune, just outside Forfar, was struck by lightning while sheltering from a storm beneath a tree. I never learned what happened to the tree but it left Willie with a blue tinge to his complexion for the rest of his life. Young Willie had been sent out by his father to inspect a potato crop when the storm broke. He was accompanied by the farm grieve (foreman) who was carrying a graipe (a twelve-tined agricultural fork) over his shoulder. The prongs of the fork were struck by the lightning and the man was sadly killed.

Thunderstorms have been a keynote of some of our most memorable family holidays. Returning from camping on Benbecula, we stopped for a night at my best man's farm of Swordale, outside Evanton. We pitched the tent close to a large elm and, in the dark hours, thunder rent the air and forks of lightning stabbed the opposite side of the glen. Despite the Doyenne's gloomiest predictions, the elm tree did not crash upon us, prematurely wiping out our 'babies' but the tent let in water and we were a sodden bunch by the morning!

When holidaying in a French country cottage, our sleep was riven by wild claps of thunder and great sheets of lightning of an electric storm. The headboard on the bed was tinplate but painted and grained to look like wood. The Doyenne decided this would attract the lightning and she resolutely prepared to meet her fate. I pointed out that the flashes would have to bend to get through the small low window and then turn left but nothing I said would calm her until she surprised herself by surviving the ordeal.

The powers of nature are no respecters of persons. The Doyenne and I were guests at the royal garden party at the Palace of Holyroodhouse, where, it seemed, half the county of Angus had gathered to join the celebrations for the Queen's eightieth birthday. As Her Majesty stepped out of the palace, the heavens opened and rain descended in traditional stair rods on a sea of expensive hats and even more costly outfits. Not content with this, great claps of thunder boomed above us and jagged forks of lightning clove the sky.

It seemed as though the happy event might be a washout. Safe beneath my umbrella (how wise of the Doyenne to suggest that I should take it), we joined in the general exasperation at the fickle weather. But not for long – I suddenly understood nature's subtle intervention. The thunderous peals of celestial applause were the accompaniment to a lightning display of festive pyrotechnics for Her Majesty. Right on cue, nature had got it right.

August – Swimming Moles

It must have been a particularly successful breeding season for buzzards for we are nearly driven demented by their incessant, keening cries round the house. They're handsome birds to look at but their whining, repetitive call is quite at odds with their fierce appearance. I can't think that there's enough feeding to support them all so perhaps some will move on simply to survive.

By comparison, the three herons, which landed at the stream that runs through the garden, were a lot more notable. I've seen four or five in a field following the plough when there's plenty of grubs and beetles being thrown up but the stream holds very little that might interest these birds – which probably explains why seeing even one is a bit of an event.

Still on birds . . . despite thinking that the hen swallow had deserted her eggs, a second brood of swallows at the front door porch has successfully hatched. At least three gaping beaks can be seen stretching up for food each time one of the parent birds lands at the nest.

Global warming has a lot to answer for. The heatwave may have been welcomed by many but most definitely not by Macbeth and Inka. The two of them have stayed firmly indoors for the past month, only going out when it was walk time. We had to bring forward Macbeth's regular three-month clip because he was so uncomfortable under his mat of hair.

Hot days mean warm evenings. The Doyenne and I joined a host of friends for an annual barbecue on Lunan Bay beach between Montrose and Arbroath. We drove home in the gloaming over Maryton Hill which has wonderful views across Montrose Basin to the foothills of the Grampians. The lights of the town were reflected in the water and the hills stood out inky black in the dusk with the light behind them. We spotted a farmer using every available hour to get the harvest underway. As we paused on the brow of the hill, we watched the lights of his combine harvester as it crawled over the land like some monstrous horniegolloch (earwig).

The Doyenne and I went to pick geans (wild cherries) from a wee stand of the trees by the side of the River North Esk. We've never seen such a profusion of fruit, even in orchards in France when on holiday. In about forty minutes, we picked fifteen pounds and now the problem is knowing what to do with them all.

I'll end this 'sack of shakings' with a fishy story to test the limits of your credulity. Son Robert was fishing in Perthshire and one of the party caught his first-ever fish – a four-pound pike. When he opened it up to clean it, out popped a dead mole. I know – I cast my eyes heavenwards too. Most folk know you don't get swimming moles as far north as Perthshire!

Autumn

Early September - Church Raptor

Macbeth is the most fair-weather dog I know. He's lying out on the grass soaking up the sunshine. It's not as blisteringly hot as it was in July and the temperature is about right for him with his 'hairy jumper'. Inka is lying not far off. His coat is shiny and he's looking the picture of health.

I know what will happen next – one of them will decide it's time to come back indoors again. There will be an unseemly rush to see which can get to the knee-hole of my desk first and squeeze in below it and lie on my feet. It's very cosy when there's just one. When both insist on creeping in, I end up typing at arm's-length and (the curse of short sight) not quite able to read what I've typed.

I had a welcome meeting with Ben Reid, known to a generation of Montrosians as 'the meter man', from the days when he called at houses each quarter to read the electricity meter. He told me about the peregrine falcon which has taken up residence high up in the Old Kirk steeple which dominates Montrose. It's been seen there for about two years now and seems to be established permanently. I went to have a look for myself, hoping to see it. It's surprising how quickly you can gather a little crowd round about you if you stand staring intently skywards. Everyone wants to know what you can see that they can't.

I didn't see the bird but I saw evidence of a recent meal. In a corner of the church were the remains of a tern. Just two fully feathered wings connected by a skeleton which had been picked quite clean. Close by was a pellet, or dropping, which had small feathers sticking out of it.

I phoned Rev. Laurence Whitley, minister of the church, who told an amusing little story against himself. When the peregrine first took up residence and left its victims' skeletons lying around the church precincts, his first thoughts were that some voodoo cult might be targeting him and his church. He was greatly relieved to find out that the reason was very much more prosaic and natural!

Peregrines are essentially birds of moorland and open spaces but moving to a town address more or less assures a ready supply of pigeons and garden songbirds for tea. Our Montrose peregrine also has the shoreline to hunt its prey, as well as the terns which nest and roost within the Glaxo Wellcome factory site.

During both world wars peregrines were shot and trapped because it was believed they posed a danger to military carrier pigeons. They are amongst the fastest birds in the world, reaching speeds in excess of 120 mph when diving, or 'stooping', on their prey. At that speed, the victim's death on impact is instantaneous.

Late September - Prisoner in a Jelly Factory

HELP! I'm a prisoner in a jelly-making factory.

I should have seen it coming when the Doyenne collected the windfall apples from the garden for her rowan and apple jelly, which is the perfect accompaniment to roast venison and pheasant. But I let my attention wander.

After I'd picked the four and a half pounds of brambles I should have gathered up my scattered wits as well. And when the bags of sugar appeared it was my last warning.

'Double, double, toil and trouble' – I can understand how Macbeth (not our 'demented ball of string' but the king from Shakespeare's Scottish play) felt on his midnight fling with the three witches. 'Cauldron bubble' – I know all about that too. Dark, steaming brews foaming and writhing in the jelly pan. My worst fears will be confirmed if the Doyenne casually asks for 'tongue of dog' to add that final extra zing. The dogs and I will be heading for the hills!

Grandchildren Cecily and Fergus call brambles 'purple treasure', which seems a thoroughly apt name. I picked the berries just in time for they were starting to spoil with the rain of the previous few days. It has been a good year for them and the jelly set perfectly when it was poured into the jars. The remainder of the fruit was frozen, to be used at Christmas in bramble and apple pies.

My travels take me to some interesting places. I got the chance to see round a remarkably well-preserved early-Victorian stable block. It's never been put to another use, which has been the saving of it. The four loose stalls are lined throughout, ceiling and all, in pine. No one knows how long ago the last horse was led out but the comfortable smell of horses is ingrained in the wood. Even in the dark you would know exactly where you were. I can imagine the last stable boy coming back and finding the stables just as he left them.

Next door is the tack room with wooden pegs, set high on the wall, for the harness and seats for the saddles. Cast-iron heating pipes run into the tack room but they don't go as far as the stables – presumably the horses were expected to generate their own warmth. The heating came from what was obviously the garage because it has an inspection pit in the floor, which is covered over with thick planks. In the early motoring days, chauffeurs were expected to be mechanics as well and the inspection pit had the same purpose as modern hydraulic ramps.

Sadly, for the horse, the invention of the motor car marked the beginning of its end as the accepted means of travel. The car became 'the real way to travel! The only way to travel!' Ask Mr Toad in *The Wind in the Willows*.

From the Doyenne's Kitchen

Of all the jams and jellies, I think bramble jelly is the most delicious and, having a devoted bramble picker in your household, immune to bramble thorns, is a distinct advantage. I also freeze them and put a handful in with apples for bramble and apple pie made with my sweet shortcrust pastry (see p. 177). Wild raspberries are also delicious mixed with apples in a pie or crumble.

Rather than giving your supper party hostess the usual box of chocolates or the bottle of wine you didn't like the look of when it was presented to you, it is much more satisfying to take something home-made with you. Bramble jelly is always welcome – at home or away.

BRAMBLE JELLY

4 lbs brambles
juice of 2 lemons
¼ pint water
sugar

Method

Pick over the brambles, put them in a pan with the lemon juice and water and cook for about an hour until the fruit is really soft. Strain through a jelly cloth.

Measure the strained liquid and return to the pan, adding a pound of sugar for each pint of liquid. Stir until the sugar has dissolved and boil rapidly until a 'jell' is achieved on testing. Skim, pot and cover in the usual way – then hide or your husband will eat it all!

October – Low Fungi and Tall Trees

Mushrooms . . . Toadstools . . . Some folk used to say 'puddockstools' but a puddock is a frog (I've sometimes seen it spelt 'paddock') and you don't get 'frogstools'. It must all get a bit confusing if you didn't grow up in *Courier* country. What started this line of thought is the tremendous amount of fungi that has appeared in the woods this year.

I grew up believing that mushrooms are edible but toadstools are poisonous. I don't actually know how to distinguish between the two despite reading a splendid little book called *Edible Fungi* by John Ramsbottom, from which it seems that many toadstools are indeed edible. The Bible refers to 'leprosy of a house' which apparently is the dry rot fungus and probably best left out of your diet or your wooden leg may fall off.

Out with the dogs, I came across a most colourful fungus at the foot of a monkey puzzle tree. Monkey puzzles are uncommon enough even in old country gardens laid out with exotic trees and this fungus was new to me. Checking in the book, it seems, from its bright coral pink lobes, to be salmon salad and, from a distance, it was certainly suggestive of a slice of cold salmon on a plate.

The noise of chain saws in nearby woods caught my attention and I had to go and investigate. It was two tree surgeons being assessed for the top qualification in tree surgery. They were from Scottish and Southern Energy (Hydro Electric to you and me) and their job is to keep power lines free from potential branch damage and help maintain continuous electricity supply, as well as protect the public.

It's a very physical job and I watched them climbing trees with – ropes although they sometimes use climbing irons strapped to their boots. Health and safety and protective equipment are primary considerations, which is not surprising when you consider the heights they work at. Chain saws revolve at the equivalent of over 50 mph so there's little time for second thoughts when you're forty feet up and the only things stopping you falling off your perch are your safety harness and climbing rope.

The arboriculture industry looks to prolong the life of trees, especially amenity trees, and tree surgeons have to be aware of matters such as tree ownership, planning and legal constraints and tree preservation orders. It was interesting to learn that the job also requires knowledge of such things as ground site fungi which attack root systems and make trees unstable – and ready for the chop. So it's certainly not a case of 'I'm a lumberjack and I'm all right' as the Monty Python song goes.

And should you take a fancy for some mushrooms, pay heed to Mr Ramsbottom who advises against eating too much of any fungi at once. Doing so, he says, may result in 'wishful reflection'. His safeguard against 'accidents' is a hen-dung and vinegar emetic!

Early November - Scotland Invented Whisky

Dogs, Doyenne and I are all back from an autumn break on the west coast. We chose a dreadful week, weather-wise, that affected pretty well the whole of Scotland. That said, although it rained stair rods much of the time, we didn't have the terrific winds that affected the eastern counties, with fallen trees and other damage.

As H. V. Morton wrote in *In Scotland Again*, 'Rain fell all day with the nagging persistence of toothache . . . The sky fell. The earth gushed water . . . it was made perfectly clear why Scotland invented whisky.'

At the beginning and end of the week, we were joined by congenial friends who cheerfully shared the weather's vicissitudes. We managed walks in the breaks in the weather and the rest of the time we sat indoors and defied the worst that the elements could throw at us. It's surprising how much you can defy sustained by a steady supply of conginiality and tonic! Conginiality and tonic! The Doyenne claims I make the best gin and tonic in the world.

Recipe for the best G&T in the world
a rummer or large tumbler (this is not a drink for sipping)
ice cubes
lemon

gin – my preferred brands are Gordon's and Plymouth
Schweppes Indian tonic water

Method

Pour a generous splash of gin on to 3 or 4 ice cubes and
leave for 10 minutes to cool the spirit and drive off the
ill humours. Add a generous squeeze of lemon juice.
Top up, right to the top of the glass, with tonic. Drink
while the bubbles from the tonic are still rising in the
glass and the taste buds are at their most receptive.

Son Robert, who claims to know a thing or two about
such matters, gave us a useful piece of advice. If you use
supermarket own-brand tonic water, squeeze lime juice
to taste instead of lemon.

Few people have tasted the perfect G&T. The
strength of will needed to wait ten minutes seems to be
an insuperable hurdle!

From the Doyenne's Kitchen

Out of doors on a wet and windy day, nothing warms
the cockles better than sloe gin – what my father-in-law
used to call a hedgerow cordial, as if it was an innocent
non-alcoholic refreshment!

Most people I know jealously guard the whereabouts
of their sloe bushes, which in reality are blackthorn
bushes, so take advantage of the spring weather, when
the blossom is on the branches, to track down your own
special supply of the fruit for the autumn.

SLOE GIN

1 lb sloes
3–4 oz granulated sugar
1½ pints gin

Method

Tradition says you should pick sloes only after the first of the autumn frosts as you can be sure they are fully ripened by then. Climate change and global warming have probably scuppered that convention but you should normally expect to pick them between mid October to mid November. If you can't use the sloes straight away, they freeze well.

Stalk and clean the sloes and prick them all over with a darning needle to help release the juice. (If they've been in the freezer they don't need pricked.) Put them into a bottling jar with the sugar and the gin. Close tightly and leave in a dark place for three months. You should shake the bottle(s) to help dissolve the sugar. Do this each day for a fortnight, then every second day for the next fortnight and once a week for the next two months.

Strain through a muslin, pour into bottles with screw tops or corks and leave until desired – which usually isn't very long when the word gets out! However, if you can manage to hide one bottle for a year before drinking it, the sloe gin will have matured and have a wonderful mellow taste.

Inka has boundless energy and the ancient oak woods down on the Kintyre peninsula were perfect for walking him – thick, overgrown and hard to get through once you get off the established paths. He ran several dozen times further than we walked and was happily tired by the end of the day.

By contrast, Macbeth was much more circumspect. His short legs are for taking him down fox holes for West Highland terriers were bred originally as hunting dogs to flush foxes out of their dens to be destroyed. He sees little sense in careering about the countryside when that's not his purpose in life. Macbeth was, in fact, back in his spiritual home. The West Highland white terrier breed we know today was developed in the early 1900s by a Colonel Malcolm of Poltalloch, an estate about a dozen miles from where we were staying. The impact of history and significance of it all were totally lost on 'himself'.

We took a drive up to Ballachulish, which lies at the foot of fateful Glencoe. There's a road bridge now at Ballachulish but I well remember the anticipation of driving on to the ferry which crossed the narrow neck of Loch Leven. It was a break in the journey for a wee laddie and I was allowed out of the car for a breath of fresh air. There were warnings of dire consequences if I went too near the side of the ferry, especially if I was careless enough to fall overboard.

It was one of some dozen ferries that saved drivers long and wearisome detours round winding sea lochs which plunge inland from the coast. The bridges over these crossings speed up journeys and are a boon to tourism but a bit of the romance of driving down the west coast was lost as, one by one, the ferries were discontinued.

Late November - Recycling the Biker

There's no denying now that winter's on its way. We woke up to the first morning with frost on the cars and we had to run them for some minutes to let the heaters clear the windows.

Perhaps it's time I tried out my new bike and worked up a bit of a healthy glow. A thoughtful minister's wife gave it to me because it was excess to her family's needs. The offer seemed a grand chance to improve my fitness and enjoy some added togetherness with the grandchildren when they come to visit. I'm not so certain now.

I can't think when I last took to the high roads on a bicycle. Like swimming, riding a bike is something you don't forget but you certainly get rusty.

I pumped up the tyres and tested the brakes. With a foot on one pedal and giving myself several 'punts' with the other foot to get moving, I swung my leg resolutely over the saddle. After the initial wobbles and much wild correcting with the handlebars, I was off. My first reaction was that they surely made bicycle seats a lot comfier in the past. I seemed to be sitting on a very narrow plank which was reminding me of parts of me that hadn't seemed important for some time. And where was the Sturmey-Archer three speed gear change? This bike has seven gears, which is nearly rocket science – and I'm not ready for that.

I rather thought that by walking two dogs every day, as I do, my legs would be in good shape for pedalling. Not so – the muscles may be in great shape for walking but you use them in a totally different way when cycling and I was soon toiling up even the slightest incline.

Could another problem be that my centre of gravity seems to have slipped southwards rather alarmingly? A neighbour who has had both hips replaced is just a blur on the horizon as he races round the countryside on his bike so there has to be hope for me.

As I lurched off up the drive, the dogs sat down in baffled horror at what the beloved master was up to this time. I was away for six or seven minutes and, when I got back, they were both still sitting, stunned, where I had left them.

So, if you are driving between Brechin and Edzell and see a figure on a pushbike, wavering uncertainly across the road, give him a wide berth. It might be me and I shouldn't have been let out unaccompanied until the grandchildren have given me a few lessons on road safety.

Despite the frosty nights and approaching winter there are flowers on the wild strawberries planted in the old troughs at the front door. It's all getting topsy-turvy. I don't expect to see them until May.

2006 – 2007

Winter

Early December - Nature, the Great Provider

I can't remember how the conversation got round to nature's more off-beat liberality but, when I mentioned that my mother used to cook me and my father rook pie, it was clear from the raised eyebrows and faint looks of distaste that this was not a subject for the breakfast table. Mother used only the breasts from juvenile birds before they had learnt to fly. At that age their diet is mainly seeds and grain and other vegetable matter and the meat is tender.

In the past it was a way for folk to add protein to what, for some, could be pretty indifferent daily fare. It was taking a harvest from what was available, like rabbits and hares or squabs which are fledgling pigeons.

I was told recently about a girl who drives north on the A9 to visit her Caithness auntie. She rarely returns home empty-handed, picking up various birds and animals that have met an untimely end with the traffic on that busy road. She puts them to good use and I can't think of better examples of Scottish thrift than her aptly named 'A9 soup' and 'A9 stew'.

I readily admit to bringing home 'roadkill' myself. A dead pheasant isn't going to grace the countryside any more so what more fitting end for it than gracing my supper plate? I just got to it before the crows did.

Ducks would seem to be as great opportunists as us humans. I joined a farmer friend to walk round a part of his farm which has a couple of wee ponds. He told me that, in the spring, mallard come to the ponds to feed on frogspawn. To give all the wannabe frogs some chance of a future, he lays chicken wire over the spawn to ward off the predators.

I remember in the 1950s a gamekeeper near Ullapool telling my father and me that mallard are carnivorous. When he gutted rabbits which he had trapped, he threw the paunch into a stream. The duck were greatly attracted to this carrion treat. As I left my farmer friend, he gave me a handful of home-grown chillis. He suggested that the Doyenne might use a few to make chilli sherry. Like pink gin, this sounds as though it might be a throwback to the glory days of officers' messes in the Indian Army.

You just add four chillis to a bottle of good fino sherry and leave for up to a month – couldn't be simpler. Used sparingly, it will add zing and pizzaz to soups and the Doyenne thought it would go well thrown into stir-fry. But mark the bottle clearly. It has a kick like a drink-maddened mule and is definitely not something to be taken by the glassful. Thinking about it, a drop or two might pep up rookie pie!

From the Doyenne's Kitchen – Reluctantly!

ROOK PIE

An old recipe says, 'Only young rooks are fit to eat'. Well, I would question that. I only made rook pie once and I haven't been tempted to repeat it in a hurry – despite my husband's blandishments!

6 young rooks
¾ lb rump steak
¼ lb butter
½ pint stock
ready-made puff pastry

Method

Skin the rooks and take off the breasts. One (Scottish) recipe says you should cover the breasts with a thin strip of steak and arrange in a pie dish with butter. You then add the stock then put on the pastry. Another (English) instructs you to stew the birds to partly cook them and then let them cool. You then lay a beefsteak on the bottom of the dish and place the birds on it.

Pour 'a good deal' of melted butter thickened with flour and thinned with stock over them. Cover with flaky pastry, brushed with beaten egg, and 'bake in a good oven for 1½ hours'.

Mid December - Goose Fever

The dogs and I were walking round a lonely pond which frequently attracts duck, especially in the evening. We'd reached the top end when I heard the first haunting cries of geese heading our way. I was completely out in the open when a pack of about thirty birds flew low over our heads and landed at the far end of the pond. That surprised me for geese are usually very wary and will veer off and circle round if there's anything unfamiliar. But a strong west wind was blowing and these birds seemed determined to reach the shelter of the tree-fringed water, come what may.

As we moved on, I heard more geese and saw a huge skein coming in from the east, possibly from Montrose Basin. All I could do was curl up on the grass and call the dogs in to lie beside me. I've no experience of counting geese in the air but I tried to get some calculation of numbers passing over me. I firmly believe that somewhere in the region of a thousand geese – mostly pink-foot – flew in to join the earlier birds.

Ringing carillons from the north announced the approach of more geese. Thereafter it was quite wondrous.

In the space of a quarter hour or so, a further four colossal skeins, each as big as the first, spiralled noisily in. There must be a celestial bush telegraph that tells them all where the party is!

Their noisy clamour blotted out all other sounds and, as they settled, they passed on gossip of where the best feeding could be found and how the weather was up north. It brought back memories of times as a youngster out with my father, I would watch similar sights at dusk as great rafts of geese lifted off Montrose Basin to fly to their feeding grounds.

We lay for half an hour in the deepening mirk. The rain had started and my backside was soaking wet. Macbeth was shivering – whether from cold or excitement I couldn't tell – and it was getting pretty dark for finding our way through the wood and back to the road.

As soon as we moved, the nearest birds took fright and rose from the water. A medley of alarm and indignation crescendoed as we skirted the pond and were spotted by lookout birds. Suddenly the world erupted with a roar of powerful beating wings and a babel of harsh, condemning cries, as hundreds and hundreds of jostling geese took flight. The real wonder is that not one bird collided with another in such a confined area. Each found its own air space in the bedlam of noise and confusion.

Then there were just the receding calls of departing geese growing fainter. It was one of those intense, emotional contacts with nature that happens only rarely.

Late December - Twitcher

I sat, unusually without two dogs at my side this time, by the side of a disused quarry, one of dozens that dot the countryside. Some are so small they were obviously only opened to provide the stone for a nearby farmhouse and possibly a couple of cottar houses, before being abandoned for a more ready supply of building material.

I was looking down on the roofs and spires of Forfar and then away westwards to the hills which march down the strath of the River Tay to Perth. There was still warmth in the afternoon sun, I was sheltered from the wind and I just had the sounds of the countryside to keep me company.

What caught my attention was a party of four long-tailed tits feeding up for the night. Once the temperature dropped, they would need all the sustenance they could get to see them through to the morning. With their butterball bodies and long tails, they looked like wee, feathered lollipops, industriously working their way round scrub bushes and chattering away to each other, nineteen to the dozen, with their high 'tsi-tsi-tsi' calls. I spent fully twenty minutes quietly sitting and watching and the birds weren't in the least fazed by me being so close.

In the past, I'd have given them little more than a passing glance. Then I realised how much I was missing so now I make the most of these opportunities. They don't happen every day and I want the memories and to be able to share them.

As the weather hardens, flocks of pigeon are coming down to feed amongst the beech mast. In years past, when fields of turnips and kail and other greentops were more common and stubble fields were left unploughed for longer, they would have had a wider choice of food throughout winter.

The light was fading as the dogs took me out for the afternoon walk. Out of the dusk bounded three black Labs and my two bounced up to greet them. At first I didn't recognise the figures, happed up against the weather, who followed. All was well – friends. Their young puppy looked shiny and sleek – as well he might. He had consumed two days' worth of food that the lady of the hoose had just finished cooking. It fair put Inka in a better light!

One of the Christmassy things I look forward to is tangerines. The Doyenne tells me she can get clementines and satsumas and mandarins but tangerines, there are none. Where have all the 'tangers' gone?

It's mince pie time when the Doyenne appears with a smudge of flour on her nose. But, when the kitchen gets hot and she gets bothered and the unseasonable language starts, I find it best to shimmer out of range and escape to write my piece for Saturday.

From the Doyenne's Kitchen

MINCE PIES

In Scotland, they are still sometimes called mincemeat pies. There are two secrets to good mince pies – good mincemeat and good pastry.

I make my own mincemeat from my mother's recipe, which was certainly her mother's and I don't know how many generations before that.

'How can you be bothered to make mincemeat?' friends ask.

Well, a) it's so easy and b) it's so much nicer than the bought stuff.

For the mincemeat:
1 lb suet
1 lb currants
1 lb raisins
½ lb dates – chopped into small pieces
½ lb sultanas
½ lb mixed peel (originally candied peel which had to
  be cut by hand)
1 nutmeg, grated fresh, or 1 tsp ground
2 lbs Bramley apples – peeled, cored and grated
2 lbs sugar
juice and rind of 3 lemons
rum

Method

Put the dry ingredients into a large mixing bowl. Add the grated apple, sugar, lemon zest, juice and a lacing of rum and mix well. I leave this covered for about a week so that the sugar dissolves, the apple softens and the mixture becomes very juicy. I then decant the mixture into jam jars.

This makes a lot of mincemeat – enough for about 200 mince pies – and it always gets used up in this house!

For the sweet shortcrust pastry:
4 oz Trex
4 oz margarine
4 oz castor sugar
1 lb self-raising flour
1 egg, beaten
cold water

For the pies:
12-hole bun tins
3" round cutter
2¼" round cutter
pastry brush
Trex to grease bun tins
A food mixer

My Yorkshire mother used Trex and I always use Trex because it is the lightest type of fat you can buy. The self-raising flour is a tip I picked up from Fanny Cradock's TV cookery series many years ago.

Method

Cut Trex and marg into small squares and put into the mixer bowl. (I don't think I'd bother to make pastry if I didn't have my 40-year-old Kenwood mixer!) Add flour and sugar and beat until you have the texture of breadcrumbs. Add half the beaten egg and enough water to bind the mixture. I roll out a quarter of the mixture at a time. Liberally flour the rolling surface and roll out the pastry as thinly as possible.

Cut 12 x 3" rounds and push them into the well greased bun tins making them still thinner by pressing the bottom so that the pastry comes right up the sides.

Place a heaped teaspoonful of mincemeat into each case and run a wet pastry brush, or a wet finger, round the cut edge of the pastry. Cut 12 x 2¼" rounds and press them gently on top of the mincemeat. Brush with beaten egg, make two V-shaped cuts in the middle of each one and cook in a hot oven – 200°C or gas mark 6 for about 10 minutes or until the pastry is golden brown. Cool for 2 minutes then lift the mince pies out of the tins on to a cooling rack. Keep an eye on them or someone may come along and pinch them!

This quantity of pastry makes around 50 mince pies.

Early January - Cool Pictish Reverie

New Year heralds the turn in the road. Imperceptibly the mornings get lighter and the evenings lengthen out. We still have to get through February, which can sometimes seem like the 'dreip' on the end of winter's nose, but I've been anticipating the sense of regeneration that is evident all around. Wildlife shares the spirit of expectancy. High in the bare branches of the beech trees, jackdaws, and rooks are winking and nodding at each other, as if to say it is time to give the old nest a good 'redd up' (spring clean). They tend to return to the previous year's nests, repairing them for each new breeding season.

A friend called to tell me about McNaught's Comet which could be seen this past week in the early evening, low in the south-west sky. I know so little about the stars that I was keen to see it. So the two bold boys and I climbed the White Caterthun, the Pictish hilltop fort north of Brechin, where we could be sure of a clear view.

The setting sun drifted into dusk. Charcoal grey clouds streaked with gold and orange and ochre were eddying about in the sky. The temperature dropped as the sunset faded and nose, ear tips and cheeks felt a bit nippy. There wasn't a breath of wind and noise travelled further on the frosty air.

A raggedy chevron of geese flew south at much the same height as ourselves heading, maybe, for Forfar Loch. Below us, where the West Water runs, there was a sharp exchange of opinion between two cock pheasants. A dog barked, cattle were bawling for their tea, a flight of mallard duck, seeking their evening feed, sped by on rapid wings. Grouse barked out their distinctive call, 'go back, go back, go back' – it was the only bit of sense I heard!

Sadly the clouds didn't clear to let me see the comet, which I'd been told has a distinct, fiery tail. After more than an hour, I was perished and readily bade farewell to the elusive Mr McNaught and his comet, which probably won't turn up again for years. When I tried to stand, it felt like all my hydraulics had seized up – the dogs thought it was a great game to see me stumbling about on the dark hilltop.

One thing's for sure, if I'd been a hairy wee Pict when the Caterthuns were being built, with only my bearskin to keep me warm, I'd have been a fair-weather Pict. I'd have opted out of the winter activities and enjoyed my beaker of heather ale in front of a roaring fire in a cosy cave, well protected from the chilly weather.

As it was, when I got home I downed a couple of large glasses of sherry – it's the best remedy I know to chase away the cold.

Late January – Burns Night and Dancing Haggis

Sometimes there's a bit of happenstance about coincidence, if you know what I mean – unless you think it's all just a by-chance sort of occurrence of no real significance. I like to think that sometimes one thing leads to the next and, while there may be no earth-shattering consequence, for a brief moment a connection has been made.

Last week, I wrote about D. K. Broster's *The Flight of the Heron* and the fate of the unfortunate heron that was shot. The following Saturday morning, I saw two of the grey birds rise off flooded ponds at the back of Balgavies (pronounced Balguys) Loch on the road from Forfar to Friockheim. Neither was shot, I hasten to say, but was it coincidence that I was in the right place at the right time?

As I had driven over the Bridge of Dun earlier that morning I saw a single swan puddling about in the field by the riverside. On the Sunday afternoon, the Doyenne and I watched the TV production of the Mariinsky Ballet dancing *Swan Lake* to Tchaikovsky's much-loved music.

That took me back to my schooldays when I played the cello. My teacher was Chester Henderson who was the leading Scottish cellist of his day. Drawing the two strands of thought together took me down another memory 'dreel' (lane).

Anna Pavlova, possibly the most famous prima ballerina of classical ballet, made the 'Dying Swan' sequence from *Carnival of the Animals* by Saint-Saëns her signature dance. It expressed the bird's battle for life and its eventual death. Whenever Pavlova danced her famous solo in Scotland, she insisted that Chester Henderson played the cello accompaniment.

Dancing was on the menu when the Doyenne and I were lucky enough to get a couple of the last tickets for the Tarfside WRI (Women's Rural Institute) annual Burns Supper, which counts amongst the notable events of the social year in Glen Esk. Tarfside Masonic Hall was bursting at the seams with anticipatory salivation. The expectant company sat down to a traditional meal of home-made haggis (tell me where else you can get home-made haggis), chappit neeps and tatties. Everyone got a spoonfu' from each of four or five of the blessed creations and the main course was followed by an equally traditional sweet of clootie dumpling.

One lady 'innocently' asked me which haggis I had liked best – I wasn't falling for that one and declared them all winners!

The toasts were led by local wit and raconteur, Jim Brown, and the evening ran into the early hours with dancing and entertainment. There was a story afterwards that one of the guests hadn't managed to get out of the glen for two days. I hope it's true because it would take some of the heat off me.

The Doyenne mentioned the morning after, rather more sharply than I thought was needful, that I'd had more fun than I deserved. She was right.

February – Puzzle for the Squirrels

A red squirrel up a monkey puzzle tree? Well, in the depths of the Angus winter, I suppose you don't expect to see the monkey. It was our companion Emma who spotted it first and we all clustered round and craned our necks to see him. It was a bit too much attention and he – or perhaps it was she – shot off up the trunk to the safety of the upper branches.

Something I didn't know until I'd looked in the tree book is that monkey puzzles have an edible seed about the size of an almond. I went back to the tree to see if I could find some. I picked up plenty of the sharp, spiny leaves but, not knowing quite what I was looking for, left empty handed. Doubtless the squirrel knows the secret so what better reason to make your home in a tree which has such a ready supply of breakfasts, teas and suppers?

The day had turned into a perfect winter afternoon and the sun shone out of a flawless sky, so we – the dogs and I, that is – carried on down to the riverside walk through the blue gate at The Burn, near Edzell. At a bend of the river, at the start of the upper beat fishings, I stopped to enjoy the sunshine. The heat's gone out of it by three o'clock but the mood raised the spirits. The water sparkled and clattered down the short way to the Loups, where the rocky channel narrows and tumbles over the falls which the salmon must leap or 'loup' on their journey upstream to the river's headwaters to spawn.

There have been some lovely morning skies and sunsets over recent days. With red sky in the morning and red sky at night, it's enough to put a shepherd in a fever of indecision about what to do with his sheep. The ones grazing on the other side of the river seemed pretty contented. No doubt life is fairly routine for a sheep until someone says 'mint sauce'.

I hadn't heard of a West Dart water terrier, so called because it was bred beside the River Dart in Devon. Several of its antecedents must have had scant regard for 'the consequences' for it was an agglomeration of wire-haired terrier, Lhasa apso, Pekingese and poodle! Its most endearing characteristic was a fanatical love of water which it could scarcely be kept away from. Its owner held it in high regard, saying it looked much like an oily rag. It's dead now, so there's not much more to tell.

They say the monkey puzzle tree got its name because it would 'puzzle a monkey' trying to climb between the razor-sharp leaves. I don't think I go for that explanation. If it was true, why didn't they call it the puzzled monkey tree?